CHRISTIAN DOCTRINE IN GLOBAL PERSPECTIVE

Series Editor: David Smith

Consulting Editor: John Stott

TITLES IN THIS SERIES:

The New Global Mission, Samuel Escobar

The Human Condition, Joe M. Kapolyo

Evangelical Truth, John Stott

**CHRISTIAN
DOCTRINE
IN GLOBAL
PERSPECTIVE**

Evangelical Truth

**A PERSONAL PLEA FOR UNITY,
INTEGRITY & FAITHFULNESS**

John Stott

Series Editor: David Smith
Consulting Editor: John Stott

InterVarsity Press
Downers Grove, Illinois

InterVarsity Press
P.O. Box 1400, Downers Grove, IL 60515-1426
Internet: www.ivpress.com
E-mail: mail@ivpress.com

Second edition © John R. W. Stott, 2003. First edition © 1999 by John Stott.

Published in the United States of America by InterVarsity Press, Downers Grove, Illinois, with permission from Universities and Colleges Christian Fellowship, Leicester, England.

InterVarsity Press® is the book-publishing division of InterVarsity Christian Fellowship/USA®, a student movement active on campus at hundreds of universities, colleges and schools of nursing in the United States of America, and a member movement of the International Fellowship of Evangelical Students. For information about local and regional activities, write Public Relations Dept., InterVarsity Christian Fellowship/USA, 6400 Schroeder Rd., P.O. Box 7895, Madison, WI 53707-7895, or visit the IVCF website at <www.intervarsity.org>.

All the royalties from this book have been irrevocably assigned to Langham Literature (incorporating the Evangelical Literature Trust), a program of the Langham Partnership International which distributes books to pastors, theological teachers and students, and seminary libraries in the developing world. Further information may be obtained from, and donations sent to: John Stott Ministries, 1050 Chestnut Street, Suite 203, Menlo Park, CA 94025.

All Scripture quotations, unless otherwise indicated, are taken from the Holy Bible, New International Version®. NIV®. Copyright ©1973, 1978, 1984 by International Bible Society. Used by permission of Hodder and Stoughton Ltd. All rights reserved. "NIV" is a registered trademark of International Bible Society. UK trademark number 1448790. Distributed in North America by permission of Zondervan Publishing House.

Cover design: Cindy Kiple
Cover image: Shaun Egan/Getty Images

ISBN 0-8308-3303-X
Printed in the United States of America ∞

Library of Congress Cataloging-in-Publication Data

Stott, John R. W.
  Evangelical truth: a personal plea for unity, integrity &
faithfulness / John Stott.
      p. cm.—(Christian doctrine in global perspective)
  Includes bibliographical references (p.   ).
  ISBN 0-8308-3303-X (pbk.: alk. paper)
  1. Evangelicalism. 2. Theology, Doctrinal. I. Title. II. Series.
BR1640.S74 2005
230'.04624—dc22

2004022168

P   19   18   17   16   15   14   13   12   11   10   9   8   7   6   5   4   3   2   1

Y   20   19   18   17   16   15   14   13   12   11   10   09   08   07   06   05

Contents

Series Preface   7

Preface   9

INTRODUCTION: *Evangelical Essentials* 13

   Three Disclaimers 14

   Fundamentalism and Evangelicalism 17

   Evangelicalism's Tribes and Tenets 21

   The Trinitarian Gospel 25

   Hapax and *Mallon* 30

1 THE REVELATION OF GOD 35

   Revelation 35

   Inspiration 46

   Authority 54

   Three More Words 59

   Two Clarifications 62

2 THE CROSS OF CHRIST 67

   Our Acceptance with God 71

   Our Daily Discipleship 80

   Our Mission and Message 82

3 THE MINISTRY OF THE HOLY SPIRIT 85

    Christian Beginnings 88

    Christian Assurance 92

    Christian Holiness 96

    Christian Community 99

    Christian Mission 103

    Christian Hope 107

CONCLUSION: *The Challenge of the Evangelical Faith* 111

    Evangelical Integrity 112

    Evangelical Stability 114

    Evangelical Truth 115

    Evangelical Unity 116

    Evangelical Endurance 119

POSTSCRIPT: *The Preeminence of Humility* 122

Notes 127

Sripture Index 133

Series Preface

THIS BOOK IS ONE OF A SERIES TITLED Christian Doctrine in Global Perspective and is being published by a partnership between Langham Literature (incorporating the Evangelical Literature Trust) and InterVarsity Press. Langham Literature is a program of the Langham Partnership International.

The vision for this series has arisen from the knowledge that during the twentieth century a dramatic shift in the Christian center of gravity took place. There are now many more Christians in Africa, Asia and Latin America than there are in Europe and North America. Two major issues have resulted, both of which Christian Doctrine in Global Perspective seeks to address.

First, the basic theological texts available to pastors, students and lay readers in the Southern Hemisphere have for too long been written by Western authors from a Western perspective. What is needed now is more books by non-Western writers that reflect their own cultures. In consequence, Christian Doctrine in Global Perspective has an international authorship, and we thank God that he has raised up so many gifted writers from the developing world whose resolve is to be both biblically faithful and contextually relevant.

Second, what is needed is that non-Western authors will write not only for non-Western readers but for Western readers as well. Indeed, the adjective *global* is intended to express our desire that biblical understanding will flow freely in all directions. Certainly we in the West need to listen to and learn from our sisters and brothers in other parts of the world. And the decay of many Western churches urgently needs an injection of non-Western Christian vitality. We pray that Christian Doctrine in Global Perspective will open up channels of communication, in fulfillment of the apostle Paul's conviction that it is only *together with all the saints* that we will be able to grasp the dimensions of Christ's love (Eph 3:18).

Never before in the church's long and checkered history has this possibility been so close to realization. We hope and pray that this series may, in God's good providence, play a part in making it a reality in the twenty-first century.

John R. W. Stott
David W. Smith

Preface

NOBODY LIKES BEING LABELED. For the labels which other people stick on us are usually uncomplimentary. Their object is often to restrict us to, even imprison us in, a rather narrow stereotype. Yet labels are useful for purposes of identification, and others are sure to affix one to us if we decline to wear one ourselves. Certainly in the scientific world labels are indispensable. For some 250 years successive generations of scientists have been grateful to the Swedish botanist Carolus Linnaeus for developing his binomial system of classification.

Theological taxonomy is considerably more difficult, however! One could attempt it, I suppose. How, for example, would you label me? Perhaps "*genus*: Christian *species*: Evangelical, *subspecies*: Anglican." But one would soon get stuck. For to classify organisms according to their structure demands a high degree of precision, whereas to classify human beings according to their beliefs would be a much more flexible and fluid task. Biologists themselves are sometimes divided into "lumpers" and "splitters," according to their tendency either to unite racial forms into a single species or to separate them into several. Lumping and splitting also goes on in the Christian community. Yet both processes become unhealthy if they are taken too far. Some Christians go on everlastingly splitting until they find themselves no longer a church but a sect. They remind me of the preacher described by Tom Sawyer, who "thinned the predestined elect down to a company so small as to be hardly worth the saving."[1] Others lump everybody together indiscriminately until nobody is excluded.

Avoiding both extremes, we recognize that there is still some genuine overlap between the Catholic, liberal and evangelical streams of Christendom. Let me give two examples which, even if specifically Anglican, illustrate the point.

Michael Ramsey (archbishop of Canterbury from 1961 to 1974) called himself an Anglican Catholic. He was nevertheless committed to the gospel of justification by faith only, which, as I will argue later, is an essential evangelical belief. He went further and affirmed that during the fifty years between 1889 and 1939 "the cardinal convictions of the Reformation" were unhesitatingly held by "all typical Anglicans," namely "that works cannot earn salvation, that salvation is by grace alone received through faith, that nothing can add to the sole mediatorship of the cross of Christ, and that Holy Scripture is the supreme authority in doctrine."[2]

My second example comes from the pen of John Habgood (archbishop of York from 1983 to 1995) in his book *Confessions of a Conservative Liberal.* "Liberal" for him "represents an openness in the search for truth which I believe is profoundly necessary for the health of religion. . . . It is essentially about honesty." At the same time it is honesty "rooted in what God has given, both in revelation and in the created world. Hence 'conservative.'"[3] Although Habgood has sometimes applied to evangelical Christians the rather rude epithet *biblicist,* his sketch of the tension between the given and the open, humility and honesty, revelation and tradition, "the believing heart and the critical mind" (p. 9), is one which—at least in principle—all evangelicals should be able to endorse.

I try not to forget, therefore, in what I go on to write, that the three broad Christian schools of thought (Catholic, liberal and evangelical) are not always mutually exclusive, for along with their divergences there are points of convergence. Indeed, we rejoice and give thanks that the great majority of Christian believers affirm the Apostles' and the Nicene Creeds, and that the great majority of Protestants still affirm many Reformation truths. In other words, not all evangelical essentials are evangelical distinctives. At the same time, biblically and historically, there are some truths which evangelical Christians have always emphasized, and which they see themselves (with due modesty, I hope) as holding in trust for the rest of the church.

While preparing this edition of *Evangelical Truth* for inclusion in the Christian Doctrine in Global Perspective series, I have been conscious that most of my references belong to a British or North American context and may on that account seem inappropriate to an international readership. So I could have eliminated them. But I decided to retain them for two reasons. First, each of them makes a point which is applicable to Christians in every culture. Second, the fact is that I am white and Western, indeed English and Anglican. To forget or deny this would breach my personal integrity. Besides, readers should not have any great difficulty in transposing to their own culture what I write and quote, for *evangelical* is a noble word; it transcends culture.

Why then do I offer a new edition of this small book to a global readership? Readers have the right to expect authors to take them into their confidence regarding their reasons for writing. Is it merely that I suffer from what I believe Juvenal called the *insanabile cacoëthes scribendi* (the incurable itch to write)? I hope not. I have at least two conscious motives.

First, I continue to be profoundly grieved by our evangelical tendency to fragment. During the last half-century the evangelical movement worldwide has grown out of all recognition in numbers, church life, scholarship and leadership—but not, I think, in cohesion. Nowadays people refer to the multiple "tribes" of evangelicalism, and like to place a qualifying adjective in front of *evangelical*. There are many to choose from: conservative, liberal, radical, progressive, open, Reformed, charismatic, postmodern and so on. But is this really necessary? While holding with a good conscience whatever our particular understanding of the evangelical faith may be, is it not possible for us to acknowledge that what unites us as evangelical people is much greater than what divides us? Must we forever remain what Bishop Stephen Neill called "obstinate individualists"[4] and consequently, in the words of Archbishop Sir Marcus Loane of Sydney, "have as much internal cohesion as the proverbial rope of sand"?[5]

I am not so naive as to imagine that this little book will solve the problems of our uncertain evangelical identity or our debilitating evangelical disunity, or will provide a flag under which we can all rally. Yet I do hope and pray that it will lay some misunderstandings to rest and will help us to combine a commitment to essential evangelical truth with an authentic generosity of mind and spirit.

Second and more personal, as I approach the end of my life on earth, and as I complete more than sixty years of privileged Christian discipleship, I would like to leave behind me, as a kind of spiritual legacy, this little statement of evangelical faith, this personal appeal to the rising generation. Of course I have changed over the last six decades. Yet I hope these changes have been not the denial of anything I previously affirmed, but rather the enrichment of what was inadequate, the deepening of what was shallow, and the clarification of what was obscure. The great evangelical truths remain. This is how I would wish to be remembered and judged, as I prepare to stand before the judgment seat of Christ.

Introduction
Evangelical Essentials

THE HARVEST OF PEOPLE INTO THE KINGDOM OF GOD in recent years has been unprecedented. Never in history has such a high percentage of the world's population been exposed to the gospel, nor the increase of evangelical Christians been so encouraging." In particular, "the growth of evangelical believers in the Third World has accelerated dramatically since World War II."[1]

Yet in spite of this worldwide expansion (even explosion), evangelical believers have often suffered from a bad press, being misunderstood and misrepresented. John Peart-Binns, for example, called the popular, jolly and godly Bishop John Taylor Smith, who was chaplain-general of the British forces during the First World War, "a rabid pietistic Evangelical of the narrowest of views and most rigid of minds."[2] Canon Michael Saward tells the story of a pretty but ignorant news reporter who turned to him in Church House one day and asked, "These Evangelicals, are they . . . snake worshippers?"[3]

A bit more accurate, but still unfriendly, is David Hare's portrait of the Rev. Tony Ferris in his book and play *Racing Demon*. He attributes people's different theological views to their social class. "Educated clerics don't like evangelicals," he writes, "because evangelicals drink sweet sherry and keep budgerigars and have ducks in formations on their walls. . . . Yes, and they also have the distressing downmarket habit of trying to get people emotionally involved."[4]

Turning to the North American scene, Professor James Davison Hunter of the University of Virginia gives his readers a rich sample of contemporary slander. Leading academics, he writes, apparently describe evangelicals as "right-wing zealots," "religious nuts," "a misanthropic cult," "fanatics," "demagogues," "anti-intellectual and simplistic"; our message is considered "vicious," "cynical," "narrow," "divisive" and "irrational."[5]

What then is evangelical Christianity or the evangelical faith, which arouses such a combination of popularity and unpopularity, which on the one hand is growing so rapidly and on the other provokes so much scorn? Let me begin by telling you what it is not.

THREE DISCLAIMERS

First, the evangelical faith is *not a recent innovation*, a new brand of Christianity which we are busy inventing. On the contrary, we dare to claim that evangelical Christianity is original, apostolic, New Testament Christianity. The very same claim and counterclaim were made during the sixteenth century. The Reformers were often dubbed innovators by the Roman Catholic Church, but they refuted the accusation. It was the medieval scholastics who were the innovators, they maintained, whereas the Reformers were renovators, seeking to go back to the beginning and recover the authentic, original gospel. "We teach no new thing," wrote Luther, "but we repeat and establish old things, which the apostles and all godly teachers have taught before us."[6] Hugh Latimer, the popular preacher of the English Reformation, made the same claim: "Ye say it is a new learning. Now I tell you it is the old learning."[7] More eloquent still was the insistence of John Jewel, bishop of Salisbury from 1560, in his famous *Apology* (1562): "It is not our doctrine that we bring you this day; we wrote it not, we found it not out, we are not the inventors of it; we bring you nothing but what the old fathers of the church, what the apostles, what Christ our Saviour himself hath brought before us."[8]

The same criticism that evangelical Christians are innovators has been heard in every generation, and the same rebuttal too. John Wesley, for example, was often accused of introducing new doctrines into the Church of England. He vigorously denied it: "It is the plain old Christianity that I teach," he insisted.[9] Toward the beginning of Billy Graham's astonishing evangelistic career, he was accused not of novelty but of being hopelessly out of date, setting back the cause of religion a hundred years. Yet his rejoinder was the same. "I did indeed *want* to set religion back—not just 100 years but 1900 years, to the Book of Acts, where first century followers of Christ were accused of turning the Roman Empire upside down."[10]

Second, the evangelical faith is *not a deviation from Christian orthodoxy.* It is neither an eddy nor a backwater but mainstream Christianity. Evangelical Christians have no difficulty in reciting the Apostles' Creed or the Nicene Creed, without mental reservations, and without needing to cross their fingers while doing it. *Evangelical,* in spite of the antipathy it has aroused, is in fact a proud word with a long and honorable pedigree. It came into widespread use only in the early eighteenth century, in relation to the so-called evangelical revival associated with John Wesley and George Whitefield. But in the seventeenth century it had been applied both to the Puritans in England and to the Pietists in Germany, and in the sixteenth century to the Reformers. They called themselves *evangelici*, short for *evangelici viri*, "evangelical men," a designation which Luther adopted as *die Evangelischen.*

Even this was not the beginning, however. In the fifteenth century John Wycliffe, sometimes described as the "Morning Star of the Reformation," was called *doctor evangelicus*. Earlier still we acknowledge as proto-evangelicals all those other Christian leaders who attributed ultimate authority to Scripture and salvation to Christ crucified alone. This could include even the great church father Augustine, who proclaimed divine grace as the only remedy for human guilt. From him it is but a short step back to the New Testament itself, and to its gospel or "evangel," from which evangelical Christians derive their name.

It is in more recent church history, however, that the terms *evangelical* and *evangelicalism* became current. In nineteenth-century Britain, for example, a number of evangelical leaders gained national prominence. Charles Simeon, vicar of Holy Trinity, Cambridge, for fifty-four years (1782-1836), had an enormous influence on generations of students through his expository preaching. William Wilberforce, who campaigned for forty-five years on behalf of African slaves, along with his allies achieved the abolition first of the slave trade in 1807 and then of slavery itself in 1833. Anthony Ashley Cooper, seventh earl of Shaftesbury (1801-1885), found inspiration for his many social reforms in his evangelical convictions. And J. C. Ryle, bishop of Liverpool from 1880 to 1900, was an able, outspoken champion of evangelical truth over against the tendencies he called "Romanism" and "scepticism."

There were also prominent nineteenth-century evangelical leaders in North America. Charles G. Finney (1792-1875), for example, was committed equally to evangelism and to social reform, founding a series of "benevolent societies" for every conceivable kind of philanthropy. One of his disciples, Theodore Weld, dedicated his whole life to the antislavery struggle. D. L. Moody (1837-1899) is well known too for his effective evangelism in both Britain and America. But he was also committed to education, and his personal influence was extremely widespread. Another educator was Charles Hodge (1797-1878). A professor at Princeton Theological Seminary for fifty-six years, he not only championed evangelical orthodoxy but is said to have taught over three thousand students. Mention should also be made of the brothers Arthur and Lewis Tappan, successful businessmen who generously funded social reform, missions and evangelism, Bible distribution, Christian education and the antislavery movement.

In 1846 the so-called World Evangelical Alliance came into being in

Britain, although it was a misnomer from the start because it was a British, not an international, body. In 1951 it adopted the more modest (and more accurate) name British Evangelical Alliance and became one of the founding members of the newly founded World Evangelical Fellowship. Third, the evangelical faith is *not a synonym for fundamentalism*, for the two have a different history and a different connotation. Fundamentalism, which today is frequently used as a theological smear word, had very respectable origins. It arose from a series of twelve paperbacks titled *The Fundamentals*, which were distributed between 1909 and 1915 by Lyman and Milton Stewart, brothers from Southern California. Each booklet contained several papers by different authors. They circulated millions free of charge. The "fundamentals" included basic Christian truths like the authority of Scripture, the incarnation, the deity, virgin birth, atoning death, bodily resurrection and personal return of Jesus Christ, the Holy Spirit, sin, salvation and judgment, worship, world mission and evangelism. The word *fundamentalist* was coined to denote anybody who believed the central affirmations of the Christian faith. The authors of *The Fundamentals* were all from Britain or North America and included such evangelical stalwarts as R. A. Torrey, B. B. Warfield, A. T. Pierson, James Orr, Campbell Morgan, and Bishops J. C. Ryle and Handley Moule.

FUNDAMENTALISM AND EVANGELICALISM

Originally, then, *fundamentalist* was an acceptable synonym for *evangelical,* as for example in Dr. Carl Henry's influential little book *The Uneasy Conscience of Modern Fundamentalism*, published in 1947. In it, while complaining that "evangelical Christianity has become increasingly inarticulate about the social reference of the Gospel," he drew no distinction between fundamentalism and evangelicalism.[11] Gradually, however, fundamentalism became associated in people's minds with certain extremes and extravagances, so that by the 1950s evangelical North American leaders like Carl Henry himself, Billy Graham and Harold Ockenga were promoting what they called "the new evangelicalism" in order to distinguish it from the old fundamentalism which they had rejected.

Because of this, evangelical Christians are understandably dismayed by such books as *Fundamentalism* by James Barr and *Rescuing the Bible from Fundamentalism* by Bishop Jack Spong, which, whether from ignorance, misunderstanding or malice, perpetuate the old identification. They write as if the only choice before the church is between an enlightened liberalism and an obscurantist fundamentalism.[12] But let it be said here and now, with clarity and conviction, that the great majority of evangelical Christians (at least in Europe) repudiate the fundamentalist label because they disagree with many self-styled fundamentalists at a number of important points.

The difficulty in establishing what these points are is due to the fact that fundamentalism has never clearly defined itself over against evangelicalism or published a broadly acceptable doctrinal basis. In seeking now to do the opposite, namely to distinguish evangelicalism from fundamentalism, I shall no doubt be guilty of generalizing and caricaturing. But I ask my readers to bear in mind that what I am attempting to portray below are not identifiable individuals or groups, but certain contrasting *tendencies*. I fully recognize that my portrait of fundamentalism may fit an old-style American version, but not some of our contemporaries who retain the label while rejecting some of the substance. Similarly, my portrait of evangelicalism is idealized, for alas! some contemporary evangelicals claim the name but do not live up to the ideal.

There seem to me to be at least ten tendencies to consider.

1. Fundamentalists of the old school give the impression that they distrust *human thought*, or scholarship, including the scientific disciplines; some tend toward a thoroughgoing anti-intellectualism, even obscurantism. Authentic evangelicals, however, acknowledge that all truth is God's truth, that our minds are Godgiven, being a vital aspect of the divine image we bear, that we insult God if we refuse to think, and that we honor him when, whether through science or Scripture, we "think

God's thoughts after him," in the words of Johann Kepler.

2. In relation to *the nature of the Bible*, fundamentalists are said by the dictionaries to believe that "every word of the Bible is literally true." This is surely a slander, since the adverb *literally* is used here too sweepingly. Yet it cannot be denied that some fundamentalists are characterized by an excessive literalism. Evangelicals, however, while believing that whatever the Bible affirms is true, add that some of what it affirms is figuratively or poetically (rather than literally) true, and is meant to be interpreted thus. Indeed, not even the most extreme fundamentalist believes that God has feathers (Ps 91:4)!

3. Fundamentalists have tended to regard *biblical inspiration* as having been a somewhat mechanical process in which the human authors were passive and played no active role. Thus the fundamentalist view of the Bible, as having been dictated by God, resembles the Muslim view of the Qur'an as having been dictated by Allah in Arabic through the angel Gabriel, while Muhammad's only contribution was to take down the dictation. In this way, the Qur'an is believed to be an exact reproduction of a heavenly original. Evangelicals emphasize, however, the double authorship of Scripture, namely that the divine author spoke through the human authors while they were in full possession of their faculties.

4. In relation to *biblical interpretation*, fundamentalists seem to suppose that they can apply the text directly to themselves as if it had been written primarily for them. They then ignore the cultural chasm which yawns between the biblical world and the contemporary world. At least in the ideal, however, evangelicals struggle with the task of cultural transposition, in which they seek to identify the essential message of the text, detach it from its original cultural context, and then recontextualize it, that is, apply it to our situation today.

5. Fundamentalists tend to go beyond suspicion of *the ecumenical movement* (for which indeed there is ample justification) to a blanket, uncritical, even vociferous rejection. The most strident expression of this attitude was seen in the American Council of Christian Churches,

founded by Carl McIntyre in 1941. Many evangelicals, however, although critical of the liberal agenda and frequently unprincipled methodology of the World Council of Churches, have tried to be discerning, affirming in ecumenism what seems to them to have biblical support, while claiming the freedom to reject what has not.

6. In relation to *the church*, fundamentalists have tended to hold a separatist ecclesiology, and to withdraw from any community which does not agree in every particular with their own doctrinal position. They forget that Luther and Calvin were very reluctant schismatics, who dreamed of a reformed catholicism. Most evangelicals, however, while believing it right to seek the doctrinal and ethical purity of the church, also believe that perfect purity cannot be attained in this world. The balance between discipline and tolerance is not easy to find.

7. Fundamentalists have tended sometimes to assimilate the values and standards of *the world* uncritically (e.g., in the prosperity gospel) and at other times to stand aloof from it, fearing contamination. By no means all evangelicals escape the charge of worldliness, yet at least in theory they seek to heed the biblical injunction not to conform to this world, and are also anxious to respond to the call of Jesus to penetrate it like salt and light, in order to hinder its decay and illuminate its darkness.

8. In relation to *race*, fundamentalists have shown a tendency—especially in the United States and South Africa—to cling to the myth of white supremacy and to defend racial segregation, even in the church. Racism without doubt lingers among evangelicals too, yet there is a widespread desire to repent of it. Most evangelicals, it can be claimed, proclaim and practice racial equality, originally by creation and supremely in Christ, who broke down the walls of racial, social and sexual separation in order to create a single, united humanity.

9. Fundamentalists have tended to insist that *the Christian mission* and *evangelism* are synonyms, and the vocation of the church is simply to proclaim the gospel. Evangelicals, however, while continuing to affirm the priority of evangelism, have felt unable to sunder it from social re-

sponsibility. As in the ministry of Jesus, so today, words and deeds, proclamation and demonstration, good news and good works supplement and reinforce one another. Their separation, wrote Carl Henry, is "Protestantism's embarrassing divorce."[13]

10. In relation to *the Christian hope*, fundamentalists tend to dogmatize about the future, although to be sure they hold no monopoly on dogmatism. But they often go into considerable detail about the fulfillment of prophecy, divide history into rigid dispensations and espouse a Christian Zionism that ignores grave injustices done to Palestinians. Evangelicals, however, while affirming with eager expectation the personal, visible, glorious and triumphant return of our Lord Jesus Christ, prefer to remain agnostic about the details on which even firmly biblical Christians have differing viewpoints.

EVANGELICALISM'S TRIBES AND TENETS

While expounding my three disclaimers, I have no doubt been too negative so far. It is high time to be positive. We have considered what the evangelical faith is not. So what is it?

Before trying to answer this question, it is important to recognize that as the evangelical movement has grown throughout the world, so too has it diversified. During or after the second National Evangelical Anglican Congress, held at Nottingham University in 1977, Canon Colin Craston remarked that Anglican evangelicals were now no longer a party but a coalition.

Several attempts have been made to classify the different evangelical "tribes." In a playful mood in April 1998, the editor of the *Church of England Newspaper* suggested that there were "57 varieties of evangelicals" (corresponding to the famous fifty-seven varieties of Heinz grocery products). Rowland Croucher in Australia mentions an unnamed Californian seminary professor who claimed he could identify sixteen kinds of evangelical,[14] while Clive Calver writes about the twelve tribes of evangelicalism.[15] Other observers have reduced this number by half.

In 1975, the year following the Lausanne Congress on World Evangelization, Peter Beyerhaus of Tübingen distinguished six different evangelical groupings:

1. The New Evangelicals (including Billy Graham), who distance themselves from fundamentalism's science-phobia and political conservatism, and who strive for the greatest possible collaboration.

2. The Strict Fundamentalists, who are uncompromising in their separatist attitude.

3. The Confessing Evangelicals, who attach importance to a confession of faith and a rejection of contemporary doctrinal error.

4. The Pentecostals and the Charismatics.

5. The Radical Evangelicals, who acknowledge a sociopolitical commitment and strive to unite evangelistic witness and social action.

6. The Ecumenical Evangelicals, who are developing a critical participation in the ecumenical movement.[16]

Nearly twenty years later, in his book *Ecumenical Faith in Evangelical Perspective* (Eerdmans, 1993), Gabriel Fackre of Andover Newton School of Theology published his similar list of six categories: fundamentalists ("polemical and separatist"), old evangelicals (emphasizing personal conversion and mass evangelism), new evangelicals (acknowledging social responsibility and apologetics), justice and peace evangelicals (sociopolitical activists), charismatic evangelicals (stressing the work of the Spirit in tongue-speaking, healing and worship) and ecumenical evangelicals (concerned for unity and cooperation). It is an interesting classification of trends, some of which overlap with one another.

We still have to ask what tenets evangelical Christians have in common. For if it is true that a certain continuity of evangelical belief and practice can be traced down the centuries of church history, burning now brightly, now dimly, of what does this continuity consist? Of course there has been development, and as the challenges have changed, so have the responses. Nevertheless, most observers agree that a genuine consensus has become discernible.

In particular, a careful study of essential evangelicalism has been made by two British scholars: one a theologian and Anglican, the other a historian and Baptist.

J. I. Packer's monograph *The Evangelical Anglican Identity Problem* (1978) was a characteristically thorough "anatomy of evangelicalism." It consisted of four general claims and six particular convictions. Generally, he argued, evangelicalism is

- *"practical* Christianity"* (a lifestyle of total discipleship to the Lord Christ)

- *"pure* Christianity"*—indeed *"mere* Christianity"* (since "you cannot add to the Christian faith . . . without subtracting from it")

- *"unitive* Christianity"* (seeking unity through a common commitment to gospel truth)

- *"rational* Christianity"* (over against the popular preoccupation with experience)

Following these four general claims, Packer identified six evangelical fundamentals as follows (the headings are his, the brief parenthetical summaries mine):

1. The supremacy of Holy Scripture (because of its unique inspiration)

2. The majesty of Jesus Christ (the God-man who died as a sacrifice for sin)

3. The lordship of the Holy Spirit (who exercises a variety of vital ministries)

4. The necessity of conversion (a direct encounter with God effected by God alone)

5. The priority of evangelism (witness being an expression of worship)

6. The importance of fellowship (the church being essentially a living community of believers)[17]

About a decade later, in 1989, David Bebbington's magisterial survey *Evangelicalism in Modern Britain* was published. In it he outlined what he regarded as evangelicalism's four "main characteristics": "*conversionism*, the belief that lives need to be changed; *activism*, the expression of the gospel in effort; *biblicism*, a particular regard for the Bible; and what may be called *crucicentrism*, a stress on the sacrifice of Christ on the cross." Together these form "a quadrilateral of priorities that is the basis of Evangelicalism."[18] Derek Tidball concludes that the Bebbington quadrilateral "has quickly established itself as near to a consensus as we might ever expect to reach."[19]

We may not particularly relish Bebbington's four rather esoteric "isms," but we cannot fail to notice his selection of the Bible and the cross, evangelism and conversion, which Packer had also stressed. It illustrates Bebbington's judgment that, although evangelicalism has been continuously "moulded and remoulded by its environment,"[20] it nevertheless has "a common core that has remained remarkably constant down the centuries."[21]

At the same time, as I have reflected on these two similar lists of evangelical distinctives, I confess to a certain uneasiness. Is it altogether appropriate that an activity like evangelism, an experience like conversion and an observation like the need for fellowship, even with their theological underpinnings, should be set alongside such towering truths as the authority of Scripture, the majesty of Jesus Christ and the lordship of the Holy Spirit? They seem to belong to different categories. Perhaps I am asking for no more than a reshuffling of the cards. Yet it seems to me important, when we are trying to define our essential evangelical identity, that we distinguish between divine and human activity, between the primary and the secondary, between what belongs to the center and what lies somewhere between the center and the circumference.

For this reason I take the liberty of suggesting an adjustment. In the list of evangelical essentials proposed by Packer and Bebbington, the first three relate (deliberately, without doubt) to the three persons of the Trinity—the authority of God in and through Scripture, the majesty of Jesus Christ in and through the cross, and the lordship of the Holy Spirit in and through his manifold ministries. But the next three evangelical characteristics (conversion, evangelism and fellowship) are not so much an addition to the first three as an elaboration of them. For it is God himself, the Holy Trinity, who causes conversion, promotes evangelism and creates fellowship. It would therefore, in my view, be a valuable clarification if we were to limit our evangelical priorities to three, namely the revealing initiative of God the Father, the redeeming work of God the Son, and the transforming ministry of God the Holy Spirit. All our other evangelical essentials will then find an appropriate place somewhere under this threefold or trinitarian rubric.

THE TRINITARIAN GOSPEL

Let me put it another way. In seeking to define what it means to be evangelical, it is inevitable that we begin with the gospel. Both our theology (evangelicalism) and our activity (evangelism) derive their meaning and their importance from the good news (the evangel). And whenever we are thinking about the gospel, three fundamental questions and answers are bound to formulate in our minds regarding the origin, the substance and the efficacy of the gospel. They occur in 1 Corinthians 2:1-5, where Paul states his position over against the false teachers who were disturbing the Corinthian church.

> When I came to you, brothers, I did not come with eloquence or superior wisdom as I proclaimed to you the testimony about God. For I resolved to know nothing while I was with you except Jesus Christ and him crucified. I came to you in weakness and fear, and with much trembling. My message and my preaching were not with wise and persuasive words, but with a demonstration of the Spirit's power, so that your faith might not rest on men's wisdom, but on God's power.

The Origin of the Gospel

Question: Where does the gospel come from? *Answer:* It is not a human invention or speculation, but the revelation of God. It is not "human wisdom" (1 Cor 1:17) or "the wisdom of the world" (1 Cor 1:20; cf. 1 Cor 2:6); on the contrary, Paul calls it "God's wisdom" (1 Cor 1:24; 2:7).

There are several uncertainties about the correct translation of 1 Corinthians 2:1. Certainly Paul is describing his proclamation when he arrived in Corinth. But is he calling it a "testimony" (*martyrion*) or a "mystery" (*mystērion*)? The Greek readings are fairly evenly balanced. Also, is his genitive subjective (God's testimony or mystery) or objective (a testimony or mystery about God)? Although we are not sure how to answer these questions, it does not really matter. What does matter is that in either case Paul identifies his message as truth, indeed as revealed truth. The gospel is God's good news for the world.

The Substance of the Gospel

Question: What does the gospel consist of? *Answer:* In the eyes of the non-Christian world it is not wisdom but foolishness; not power but weakness. It does not flatter human beings. It gives us nothing to boast about. Nevertheless, it is God's wisdom and God's power. Where are these to be found, then? Only in "Jesus Christ and him crucified" (1 Cor 2:2).

We note that Paul "resolved" to proclaim nothing but Christ and the cross. This implies that he had endured a previous period of irresolution. Why was this? Sir William Ramsay popularized the theory that Paul's preceding visit to Athens had been a failure because he had preached creation instead of the cross; and that on his way to Corinth he "resolved" not to repeat his mistake. But there is no evidence that his mission in Athens had been a failure or a mistake.

Certainly Luke does not give this impression. On the contrary, he records Paul's speech to the Athenian philosophers as a fine example of his gospel approach to thoughtful Gentiles. In any case, he must have preached the cross, since he proclaimed the resurrection (Acts 17:31), and one cannot preach either without the other. Luke also tells us that there were a number of converts. So the explanation of Paul's firm decision to proclaim only Christ and him crucified was different. It is to be found not in Athens, but in Corinth; not in a past failure but in a future challenge.

Paul knew that the inhabitants of Corinth were proud, idolatrous, materialistic and immoral. He also knew that such people would not be friendly to the gospel, for the gospel of the cross is folly to the intellectually arrogant and a stumbling block to the morally self-righteous. It humbles vanity and condemns idolatry. It calls the covetous to contentment and sinners to repentance and self-denial. No wonder Paul needed to make a firm decision to limit his message in Corinth to "Jesus Christ and him crucified." Apprehensive about the reception he would get, he arrived "in weakness and fear, and with much trembling" (1 Cor 2:3).

The apostle was still focusing on the same gospel of the cross near the end of his first letter to the Corinthians, as he had been near its beginning. He made a formal statement about it:

> Now, brothers, I want to remind you of the gospel I preached to you, which you received and on which you have taken your stand. By this gospel you are saved, if you hold firmly to the word I preached to you. Otherwise, you have believed in vain. For what I received I passed on to you as of first importance: that Christ died for our sins according to the Scriptures, that he was buried, that he was raised on the third day according to the Scriptures, and that he appeared. (1 Cor 15:1-5)

Six aspects of the gospel are noteworthy.

1. The gospel is *christological*. The heart of the Christian message is that "Christ died for our sins . . . [and] he was raised." The gospel is not limited to these events, but they are its priority truths, which are "of first importance" (1 Cor 15:3). The gospel is not preached if Christ is not preached, and the authentic Christ is not proclaimed if his death and resurrection are not central.

2. The gospel is *biblical*. The Christ Paul proclaimed was the biblical Christ, who died for our sins "according to the Scriptures" and who was also raised "according to the Scriptures" (1 Cor 15:3-4). Which Old Testament Scriptures he has in mind Paul does not tell us, but no doubt they included those which Jesus used when "he explained to them what was said in all the Scriptures concerning himself" (Lk 24:25-27, 44-46), those which Peter used on the Day of Pentecost (Acts 2:25-31), and notably Psalm 22 and Isaiah 53. The first Christian evangelists made much of the fact that the death and resurrection of Jesus were corroborated by two witnesses—the prophets and the apostles, or, as we would say, the Old Testament and the New Testament.

3. The gospel is *historical*. We need to notice the reference both to Jesus' burial and to his appearances. The burial testified to the reality of his death (since we bury the dead, not the living), while the appearances testified to the reality of his resurrection. Moreover, what was raised was what had been buried. In other words, it was the body of Jesus which was raised and changed. The resurrection was also a datable historical event, since it took place "on the third day."

4. The gospel is *theological*. The death and resurrection of Jesus were not only historical events; they had a theological or saving significance. He not only died but died "for our sins." Since sin and death are related to one another throughout Scripture as an offense and its just reward, and since Jesus committed no sins of his own for which he needed to die, he must have died for our sins. The sins were ours, but the death was his. He died our death. He bore our penalty. Only thus could we be "saved" (1 Cor 15:2). This points clearly to the substitutionary nature of the cross, to which we will return in chapter two.

5. The gospel is *apostolic*. That is to say, it is an essential part of the authentic message received and transmitted by the apostles. It belongs to the apostolic tradition. In 1 Corinthians 15:11 Paul concludes, "Whether, then, it was I [Paul] or they [the Twelve], this is what we [all the apostles] preach, and this is what you [the church] believed." This

cluster of personal pronouns (*I, they, we, you*) is extremely impressive. It indicates a unity of faith between Paul and the Twelve, and between the apostles and the church, indeed between the first generation of believers and all subsequent generations.

6. The gospel is *personal.* That is, the death and resurrection of Jesus are not just history and theology but the way of individual salvation. The Corinthians had received it, taken their stand on it, and been saved by it, so long as they continued to hold firmly to it (1 Cor 15:1-2).

The Efficacy of the Gospel

Question: how does the gospel become effective? *Answer:* it does not require the contrived, flowery eloquence of the Greeks to make it work. Paul had renounced both philosophy and rhetoric. In place of philosophy he had preached "Christ and him crucified"; in place of rhetoric he trusted in the Holy Spirit. He put no confidence in his own wisdom or power. On the contrary, because of his personal "weakness, fear and trembling," he looked for "a demonstration" (*apodeixis*, "proof") of the Spirit's power.

This does not mean that Paul rejected apologetics. When he reached the Greek city of Corinth, according to Luke's account in Acts, he was still reasoning with people and "trying to persuade Jews and Greeks" (Acts 18:4). It is quite wrong to set human reasoning and trust in the Holy Spirit over against each other as if we have to choose between them. As the Spirit of truth, he brings people to faith in Christ not *in spite of* the evidence but *because of* it, when he opens their eyes to attend to it. What happened in Corinth was that he spoke in human weakness and trepidation, and the Holy Spirit took his feeble words and carried them home with divine power to the mind, heart, conscience and will of their hearers.

To sum up, the origin of the gospel was not speculation but revelation; its substance was not the world's wisdom but Christ's cross; and its efficacy was due not to rhetoric but to the Holy Spirit's power. Thus, the gospel comes from God, centers on Christ and his cross, and is confirmed by the Holy Spirit.

HAPAX AND MALLON

At this stage we need to pause and reflect. The first two of the trinity of evangelical essentials belong closely together, and there are striking parallels between them. They relate to the basic topics of every religion, namely the questions of authority (by what authority do we believe?) and salvation (by what means can we be saved?); or in evangelical terms they allude to revelation and redemption, the Bible and the cross. Both were key issues to the Reformers, who referred to *sola Scriptura* (Scripture alone for our authority) as the "formal" principle of the Reformation, and to *sola gratia* (grace alone for our salvation) as its "material" principle.

Next, both are due to the gracious initiative of God, who speaks and acts. Both focus on Christ, in and through whom God has spoken and acted. Moreover, both are *hapax* (once and for all), expressing the finality in Christ of God's revelation (his word has been spoken) and of God's redemption (his work has been done).

With regard to God's revelation, Jude wrote, "I felt I had to write and urge you to contend for the faith that was once for all [*hapax*] entrusted to the saints" (Jude 3). It was against the background of serious false teaching that Jude wrote. His readers would be able to refute them only by defending God's revealed truth which had been committed to them once and for all.

With regard to God's redemption, Paul, Peter and the writer to the Hebrews all apply the adverb *hapax* not only to Christ's first coming in general but specifically to his cross, from which he cried out in triumph, "It is finished." Here are some examples:

- *Paul:* The death he died, he died to sin once for all [*hapax*]. (Rom 6:10)

- *Peter:* Christ died for sins once for all [*hapax*], the righteous for the unrighteous, to bring you to God. (1 Pet 3:18)

- *Hebrews:* Unlike the other high priests, he does not need to offer sacrifices day after day, first for his own sins, and then for the sins of the people. He sacrificed for their sins once for all [*hapax*] when he offered himself. (Heb 7:27; cf. 9:12, 26-28; 10:10-12)

It is because we have grasped the finality of what God has said and done in Christ that we evangelical people are determined to hold both fast. It is inconceivable to us that any truth could be revealed that is higher than what God has revealed in his own incarnate Son. It is equally inconceivable that anything should be deemed necessary to our salvation in addition to the cross. To add any word of our own to God's completed word in Christ, or to add any work of our own to God's finished work in Christ, would be gravely derogatory to the unique glory of Christ's person and work. It would be to imply that God's word and work are imperfect, and that we need to supplement, improve and even perfect them. No, we are fully content with what God has said and done in Christ; he has nothing more to say or do, at least in this life.

Our critics immediately pounce on this insistence on the finality of the incarnation and the atonement. They accuse us of restricting God's saving activity to the first half of the first century A.D., and of relegating Christianity to a historical museum. "Does God have no ministry today?" they ask incredulously. "Is he imprisoned in the Bible and the cross?"

Questions like these can be asked, however, only by those who have overlooked the contemporary ministry of the Holy Spirit as the third evangelical essential. In one sense his coming too was *hapax*, for the Day of Pentecost was as unique and unrepeatable as Christmas Day, Good Friday, Easter Day and Ascension Day. That is to say, Jesus Christ was born once, died once, rose once, was exalted once and poured out the Holy Spirit once, as the final act of his saving career (Acts 2:33). Yet, although the Holy Spirit was given once and for all, to be with us "forever"

(Jn 14:16), yet his ministry is continuous and contemporary.

So the appropriate adverb to describe the Holy Spirit's activity today is not *hapax* ("once and for all") but *mallon* ("more and more"). The Holy Spirit is constantly, and indeed increasingly, showing Christ to us and forming Christ in us. The once-for-all bestowal of the Holy Spirit on the church has vital ongoing implications in relation to God's revelation and redemption through Christ. It is the Holy Spirit who, as "the Spirit of wisdom and revelation" in our knowledge of Christ (Eph 1:17ff.), opens our eyes to see ever more of what God has revealed in him.

It is also the same Spirit who enables us to inherit the full riches which are already ours through union with Christ (Eph 3:14ff.). In this way we "grow in grace," so that "from the fullness of his grace" we receive "one blessing after another" (2 Pet 3:18; Jn 1:16). Also, we "are being transformed into the same image [that of Christ] from one degree of glory to another" by the Holy Spirit (2 Cor 3:18 NRSV). The same truth of gradual transformation into the image of Christ is implied in Paul's metaphor of "the fruit of the Spirit" (Gal 5:22-23), for fruit ripens slowly, and so does Christian character. Here, then, are some Pauline verses in which the adverb *mallon* is applied to our Christian behavior.

> This is my prayer: that your love may abound more and more [*mallon*] in knowledge and depth of insight. (Phil 1:9)

> Finally, brothers, we instructed you how to live in order to please God, as in fact you are living. Now we ask you and urge you in the Lord Jesus to do this more and more [*mallon*]. (1 Thess 4:1)

> Now about brotherly love we do not need to write to you, for you yourselves have been taught by God to love each other. And in fact, you do love all the brothers throughout Macedonia. Yet we urge you, brothers, to do so more and more [*mallon*]. (1 Thess 4:9-10)

So in the two fundamental duties of pleasing God and loving one another there must be no complacency. On the contrary, we are to be constantly growing. For although our justification is *hapax* (once and for all), our sanctification is to be *mallon* (more and more).

Thus the essentials of evangelicalism may be encapsulated in the combination of the two adverbs *hapax* and *mallon*. God has spoken *hapax* in Christ (including the biblical witness to Christ), revealing himself and committing his revelation to the church. Yet our responsibility is to delve ever more deeply (*mallon*) into what he has revealed. Similarly, God has acted *hapax* in Christ, giving his Son to die for us. Yet our responsibility is to enter ever more fully (*mallon*) into the benefits of his death. God has no more to teach us than he has revealed *hapax* in Christ; but we have much more to learn, as the Holy Spirit witnesses to Christ, not least through the multicultural fellowship of the church, and so enables us to understand God's revelation ever more fully (*mallon*). And God has no more to give than he has given us *hapax* in Christ; but we have much more to receive, as the Holy Spirit enables us to appropriate God's gifts ever more fully (*mallon*).

This recognition of the need for *mallon* is well expressed in the bishop's prayer in the 1662 Confirmation Service:

> Defend, O Lord, this thy Child with thy heavenly grace, that *he* [or she] may continue thine for ever; and daily increase in thy Holy Spirit, more and more, until *he* come unto thy everlasting kingdom.

We have considered in this introduction the three essentials to which evangelical people are determined to bear witness. They concern the gracious initiative of God the Father in revealing himself to us, in redeeming us through Christ crucified, and in transforming us through the indwelling Spirit. For the evangelical faith is the trinitarian faith.[22] This is why evangelical Christians place such emphasis on the Word, the cross and the Spirit. We now devote a separate chapter to each.

Suggested Further Reading
Marsden, George. *Understanding Fundamentalism and Evangelicalism.*

Grand Rapids: Eerdmans, 1991.

McGrath, Alister. *Evangelicalism and the Future of Christianity.* Downers Grove, Ill.: InterVarsity Press, 1995.

————. *A Passion for Truth.* Downers Grove, Ill.: InterVarsity Press, 1996.

1

The Revelation of God

THE PRIMARY QUESTION IN EVERY RELIGION relates to the topic of authority: by what authority do we believe what we believe? And the primary answer which evangelical Christians (whether Anglican, Lutheran, Presbyterian, Baptist or other) give to this question is that supreme authority resides neither in the church nor in the individual but in Christ and the biblical witness to him.

The purpose of this chapter is to explore this aspect of our evangelical identity. Why do evangelicals attribute authority to Scripture? And what are the consequences of this belief? Perhaps the most helpful way to delve into the evangelical view of Scripture is to consider the cluster of three words which lie at the heart of it, namely *revelation, inspiration* and *authority.*

REVELATION

The English word *revelation,* derived from the Latin *revelatio,* an unveiling, describes an objective action by which something previously hidden by a veil is unveiled and so disclosed to view. Evangelical Christians begin their thinking with a recognition of the obvious, logical reasonableness of revelation. Since God is our Creator, infinite in his being, while we are finite creatures of time and space, it stands to reason that we cannot discover him by our own research or resources. He is altogether beyond us. And since in addition he is the all-holy God, while we are fallen, sinful and under his just judgment, there is a chasm between him and us which we from our side could never bridge. Being both finite and fallen, we cannot reach him. We could never know him (unless he should take the initiative to make himself known), and all the altars in the world, like the one Paul stumbled across outside Athens, would be inscribed "TO AN UNKNOWN GOD" (Acts 17:23). He would remain to us both incomprehensible and inaccessible.

This double fact is the basic premise of divine revelation, and a major theme of Paul's first letter to Corinth:

> For it is written: "I will destroy the wisdom of the wise; the intelligence of the intelligent I will frustrate." Where is the wise man? Where is the scholar? Where is the philosopher of this age? Has not God made foolish the wisdom of the world? For since in the wisdom of God the world through its wisdom did not know him, God was pleased through the foolishness of what was preached [the *kērygma*, the gospel] to save those who believe. (1 Cor 1:19-21)

Again,

> We speak of God's secret wisdom, a wisdom that has been hidden and that God destined for our glory before time began. None of the rulers of this age understood it, for if they had, they would not have crucified the Lord of glory. However, as it is written:
>
> "No eye has seen,
>   no ear has heard,
>   no mind has conceived
>   what God has prepared for those who love him"—
>
> but God has revealed it to us by his Spirit. (1 Cor 2:7-10)

Both these eloquent statements contrast the wisdom of God with the wisdom of the world. On the one hand, Paul declares the failure, indeed the inability, of human wisdom to find or to know God. On the other hand, he states the corresponding necessity of divine wisdom which is unattainable by the human eye, ear and imagination, but has been revealed by God, proclaimed by the apostles and is of saving efficacy to believers.

Four kinds of revelation are mentioned in Scripture. They describe the various ways in which God has revealed himself, and in some ways still does.

General or Natural Revelation

"General revelation" is so called because it is made to everybody, to the generality of humankind. It is also called "natural" because it is made through nature, through the created order. One example from each Testament will perhaps suffice.

The fullest Old Testament reference to general revelation comes in the first six verses of Psalm 19. "The heavens declare the glory of God." Their proclamation is made both continuously and universally, for their message goes out "day after day . . . night after night" and reaches "to the ends of the world," especially as the sun makes its daily circuit across the sky. And although, literally speaking, "there is no speech or language," yet metaphorically the heavens "pour forth speech." Indeed, so does the earth, for "the whole earth is full of his glory" (Is 6:3).

For the clearest statement on general revelation in the New Testament we turn to Paul and his letter to the Romans. He insists that "God has made plain" to human beings what may be known about him because throughout history ("since the creation of the world") God's invisible attributes of power and divinity have been clearly seen "from what has been made" (Rom 1:19-20; cf. Acts 14:17; 17:24-25).[1] That is, the created world is a visible disclosure of the invisible God. Just as artists reveal themselves in their art, so the Creator reveals himself in his creation. In addition, we know something of the moral order through our conscience (Rom 1:32—2:2).

Still today by creation and conscience God continues to bear witness to himself. The rationality, intricacy and beauty of the world on the one hand, and our sense of right and wrong, of duty and failure, on the other, speak to us of God. But the tragedy is that we have suppressed this truth in order to go our own self-centered way. In consequence we are guilty and without excuse (Rom 1:20; 2:1). So general revelation cannot save us; it can only condemn us. We cannot read the way of salvation in the stars. We see God's glory in the created order; for his grace we need another revelation.

Special or Supernatural Revelation

There are at least six differences between "general" and "special" revelation.

General Revelation	Special Revelation
1. It is "general" because it is made to everybody everywhere.	1. It is "special" because it was made to particular people in particular contexts.
2. It is "natural" because it is made through nature.	2. It is "supernatural" because it was made through miracle (the inspiration of the Scriptures and the incarnation of the Son).
3. It is "continuous" because it never ceases.	3. It is "final" because it was completed in Christ and the biblical witness to Christ.
4. It is "glorious" because it reveals God's glory in creation.	4. It is "gracious" because it reveals God's grace in salvation.
5. It is "visible" because through it we see God's works.	5. It is "audible" because through it we hear God's words.
6. It is "judging" because those who reject it are condemned.	6. It is "saving" because those who accept it are saved.

Of these differences, it is the second which concerns us now, namely that God's general revelation was made through nature (heaven and earth proclaiming his glory), whereas his special revelation was made through miracle (inspiration and incarnation). This combination of inspiration and incarnation is vital. We evangelicals have often made the mistake of isolating and elevating the Bible. But the climax of God's revelation was his incarnate Son, the Word made flesh: "But in these last days he has spoken to us by his Son" (Heb 1:2). The Son is further described as the agent of creation, the sustainer and heir of the universe, the radiance of God's glory and the exact representation of his being, who had provided purification for our sins and was now enthroned at God's right hand (Heb 1:1-3).

But how do we know all this about Jesus Christ? His incarnate life lasted only about thirty years, and we were not there to see it. How then could it benefit later generations and not be lost in the mists of antiquity? The answer lies in the apostles. They were chosen and equipped in order to record and explain what God had said and done through Christ. Only in that way could people in subsequent centuries have access to him. The only authentic Christ is the biblical Christ. What Scripture has done is to capture him, in order to present him to all people at all times in all places. The climax of God's revelation should be described as the historic, incarnate Christ and the total biblical witness to him.

In God's purpose of special revelation, event and testimony went together. This is important because it used to be fashionable among liberal (especially neo-orthodox) scholars to insist that God's revelation was personal, not propositional. This is a false distinction, however. God's self-revelation was indeed mostly personal—through acts of salvation and judgment. But how could such events be beneficial to those not involved in them unless there were witnesses to record and interpret the events? For example, many tribal migrations were taking place in the Middle East at the time of the exodus. How could anybody have known that Israel's exodus from Egypt was special, unless God had raised up Moses and the prophets to say so? Again, many crucifixions took place during the years that Rome occupied Palestine. How then could anybody have known that the crucifixion of Jesus was special, let alone the turning point of human history, if God had not appointed and prepared the apostles as witnesses? Thus God's special revelation was usually a combination of deed and word, event and testimony.

We should not therefore perpetuate the myth that God's revelation could be personal without being propositional too, deeds without words. We should not share in the modern disenchantment with words. Words matter. Even images need words to explain them. And God has chosen the model of human speech to illustrate his communication with us. We are familiar with such claims as these: "The word of the LORD came to me, saying . . ." (e.g., Jer 1:4). "Hear the word of the LORD" (e.g., Is 1:10). "When you received the word of God, which you heard from us, you accepted it not as the word of men, but as it actually is, the word of God, which is at work in you who believe" (1 Thess 2:13). Language is the most sophisticated means of communication we have. We cannot know each other's minds until and unless we speak to one another. We sometimes talk about "mindreading," but it is impossible. If you were to remain silent, and assume a poker face, I would not have the foggiest notion what you were thinking about. If then we cannot read each other's minds, how much less can we read God's?

"For my thoughts are not your thoughts,
    neither are your ways my ways,"
        declares the LORD.
"As the heavens are higher than the earth,
    so are my ways higher than your ways
    and my thoughts than your thoughts.
"As the rain and the snow
    come down from heaven,
and do not return to it
    without watering the earth
and making it bud and flourish,
    so that it yields seed for the sower and bread for the eater,
so is my word that goes out from my mouth:
    It will not return to me empty,

but will accomplish what I desire
    and achieve the purpose for which I sent it."
(Is 55:8-11)

Notice how the prophet moves from thoughts to words, from the thoughts in the mind to the words in the mouth. He begins with a firm statement that God's thoughts and ways are not the same as ours. Indeed, God's thoughts and ways are as much higher than ours as the heavens are higher than the earth, which is infinity. It is absolutely impossible, therefore, for us to climb up into the infinite mind of God. There is no ladder by which to reach him, no bridge by which to cross the chasm between us. If he were to remain silent, we would never know (and could never even guess) what he is thinking.

But this is not the situation, for God has spoken, the prophet continues. He makes a second reference to the heavens and the earth. Having reminded us that heaven is infinitely higher than earth, he points out that both snow and rain bridge the gap. They both "come down from heaven," and they do not return "without watering the earth." Just so, he continues, as the rain makes the earth productive, so God's word goes out from his mouth. It does not return to him empty, but accomplishes his purpose. Thus the thoughts in God's mind are inaccessible to us until and unless they are communicated by the words of his mouth, at which point they become effective in the fulfillment of his purpose.

Does this emphasis on words mean that evangelicals believe in the verbal inspiration of the Bible? Many are quick to say that they do not. They draw a distinction between the words and the sense, and like to quote the great missionary Henry Martyn. Asked in Persia by a high-ranking Muslim whether he believed in the verbal inspiration of the Bible, as his questioner did of the Qur'an, Martyn replied, "The sense is from God, but the expression [is] from the different writers of it."[1] It sounds like a useful distinction, until one examines it.

The fact is that one cannot separate the meaning of a text from the words which constitute and communicate it. Words are the building-blocks of speech. It is impossible to frame a precise message without constructing precise sentences composed of precise words. Here is what Charles Kingsley wrote in the middle of the nineteenth century:

> These glorious things—words—are man's right alone. . . . Without words we should know no more of each other's hearts and thoughts than the dog knows of his fellow dog . . . for, if you will consider, you always think to yourself in *words*, though you do not speak them aloud; and without them all our thoughts would be mere blind longings, feelings which we could not understand ourselves.

More important still, consider the claim which the apostle Paul made for himself and his fellow apostles: "This is what we speak, not in words taught us by human wisdom but in words taught by the Spirit" (1 Cor 2:13).

Progressive Revelation

To believe in divine revelation does not mean we suppose that God revealed everything to his people at once. No, he taught them gradually as they were able to assimilate it, "a little here, a little there" (Is 28:13), "in partial and various ways" (Heb 1:1 NAB). This is particularly obvious in regard to the relation between the Old and the New Testaments. Thus, the elaborate sacrificial cultus of the Old Testament had taught Israel indispensable truths, such as that atonement was made by the shedding of blood (Lev 17:11). But the animal sacrifices were discontinued in the New Testament because they had been fulfilled in the sacrifice of Jesus Christ. Wise parents do not teach their children lessons that they subsequently contradict; instead they amplify them. Otherwise they lose credibility.

Perhaps the doctrine of the Trinity is the best example. The Trinity is not explicitly taught in the Old Testament. To be sure, there are hints and adumbrations of it. When we read God's word "Let us make man" we interpret the plural as trinitarian. It is the same when we overhear the threefold shalom of the Aaronic blessing (Num 6:22ff.) or the "Holy, holy, holy" of the heavenly choir (Is 6:3; Rev 4:8). Christian ears pick up these allusions, but Jewish ears do not. For the great emphasis of the Old Testament is on the unity of God, in contrast to the crude polytheism of Israel's neighbors. For example, "The LORD our God, the LORD is one" (Deut 6:4). It was only after God's people had firmly grasped his unity that they were ready for the further revelation that he is one in three.

What we see throughout the Old Testament, Alec Motyer has written, is "a true cumulative progression." 'There is no abandonment of the early in favour of the late, the primitive in favour of the developed, but a gathering and maturing body of truth which, by the end of the Old Testament, is also truth tensed up for its brilliant dénouement."[2]

Personal Revelation

It is conducive to clear thinking when we distinguish between two ministries of the Holy Spirit and refer to them as *revelation* and *illumination* respectively. *Revelation* in this context describes an objective event, the Holy Spirit's unveiling the glory of God in nature or in Scripture. *Illumination,* on the other hand, describes a subjective event, the Holy Spirit's enlightening our eyes so that we now see what he has revealed. Both processes are indispensable if we are ever to know God.

Supposing we had met for an unveiling ceremony, for example the unveiling of somebody's portrait. Supposing too that we had invited a blindfolded person to accompany us. Before we can all see the portrait, two processes are necessary. First, the picture must be unveiled, which illustrates the objective event called "revelation." But still our blindfolded friend cannot see. A second process is necessary in his case. His bandages have to be removed, which illustrates the subjective event called "illumination." But because it involves the removal of a veil from our eyes or minds, this illumination is sometimes also called a "revelation."

Jesus himself used this language. On one occasion he thanked his Father that he had hidden his truths from the intellectually arrogant and had "*revealed* them to little children" (Mt 11:25), that is, the humble. On another occasion, when Peter first identified Jesus as the Messiah, Jesus responded, "Blessed are you, Simon son of Jonah, for this was not *revealed* to you by man, but by my Father in heaven" (Mt 16:17). What was true of Peter was equally true of Paul. His experience of conversion and commissioning on the Damascus road was so evidently due to the initiative of God's grace that he could write, "God . . . was pleased to *reveal* his Son in me" (Gal 1:15-16). And having experienced this heavenly illumination himself, he naturally desired it for others. He prayed for the Ephesians that "the Spirit of wisdom and *revelation*" would enlighten the eyes of their heart to know the fullness of God's purpose for them (Eph 1:17ff.).

Here then are four aspects of divine revelation: general and special, progressive and personal. Evangelical Christians emphasize that without revelation the knowledge of God is impossible. God himself is veiled, and so are our minds, until by his grace and power both veils are torn off. Evangelical Christians also emphasize that what God has revealed is true, and that our only reaction must be to listen, to believe and to obey.

How blessed we are that God did not abandon us to grope in thick darkness, to flounder in deep water, or even to make do with human philosophy! No, he has given us his Word as a lamp to our feet and a light for our path (Ps 119:105), indeed "a light shining in a dark place, until the day dawns" (2 Pet 1:19).

The evangelical emphasis on truth, revealed by God and therefore absolute, binding and universal, is not at all compatible with the mood of postmodernity. But then it was not compatible with the previous mood of modernity either. A Christian mind should respond to contemporary culture neither with a blanket rejection nor with an equally indiscriminate acquiescence, but with discernment. Evangelical Christians could never come to terms with modernism, that is, with the Enlightenment—its replacement of revelation with reason, its proclamation of the omnicompetence and autonomy of the human mind, and its glorification of objective science as the basis for its confidence in the inevitability of moral progress. It was high time this bubble burst, and we may be thankful that postmodernity has pricked it.

Professor Diogenes Allen of Princeton Theological Seminary has written optimistically that with the collapse of the Enlightenment vision there is now "a new possibility of God" and therefore "a new openness for faith." He shows how the four major pillars of Enlightenment confidence are all crumbling. The Enlightenment declared the following:

1. *The universe is self-contained and God is superfluous*—whereas now both philosophy and cosmology are exhibiting a new openness to God.

2. *Morality is self-evident and revelation is unnecessary*—whereas now we cannot reach a consensus for moral action or even discussion.

3. *Progress is inevitable because of science*—whereas now we are faced with our failure to solve social problems.

4. *Knowledge is inherently good*—whereas now we have to confess that knowledge is often misused for evil ends.

All this indicates that "the embargo on the possibility of God is lifted" and that the gospel has a fresh relevance.[3] And yet, alongside this new openness to faith, postmodernism is the sworn enemy of claims to absolute truth. Os Guinness describes the collision between postmodernism and modernism:

> Where modernism was a manifesto of human self-confidence and self-congratulation, post-modernism is a confession of modesty, if not despair. There is no truth, only truths. There are no principles, only preferences. There is no grand reason, only reasons. . . . If post-modernism is correct, we cannot even aspire after truth, objectivity, universality and reality.[4]

But the evangelical faith cannot capitulate to this pluralism and relativism. We must continue to argue that truth is truth. Peter Cotterell has put it well, as it confronts the Christian mission:

Truth is not a matter of pride or humility. It is a matter of fact. Islam says
Jesus wasn't crucified. We say he was. Only one of us can be right. Juda-
ism says Jesus was not the Messiah. We say he was. Only one of us can be
right. Hinduism says that God has *often* been incarnate. We say only once.
And we can't both be right.[5]

INSPIRATION

If the word *revelation* indicates that God has taken the initiative to make
himself known, the word *inspiration* indicates how he has done so, at
least in special revelation, namely by speaking to and through the human authors. In this sense the Bible is a unique book; no other book resembles it. For it is God's word through human words. It thus has a
double authorship (divine and human), which on that account demands
a double approach—reverent because it is the Word of God, "critical" (to
be defined later) because it is the word of human beings.

The Double Authorship of Scripture

Evangelical Christians are anxious to avoid the opposite extremes of fundamentalism and liberalism. So-called fundamentalists (at least of the
old school), as we have seen, declare that the Bible is the Word of God.
They tend to regard the human authors as having been entirely passive,
their human faculties having been suspended by divine inspiration.
They sometimes liken the Bible's human authors to musical instruments
or dictating machines, no longer living persons but lifeless toys in the
hand of the Spirit. So-called liberals, by contrast, declare that the Bible
is the word of human beings, originating in their minds and ennobled
by only occasional flashes of divine inspiration. But neither of these ac-
counts of Scripture will do, because neither is the account which the
Bible gives of itself.

There is a third way, best designated the double authorship of Scripture. It is both the Word of God and the word of men, indeed the Word
of God through the words of human beings. Examples abound. The Pen-

tateuch is called in the same passage "the Law of Moses" and "the Law of the Lord" (Lk 2:22-23), and Jeremiah introduces his prophecy as "the words of Jeremiah" into whose mouth Yahweh had put his words (Jer 1:1-9). Similarly, we read in the New Testament both that "God spoke . . . through the prophets" and that "men spoke from God" (Heb 1:1; 2 Pet 1:21). In consequence, it could be said equally that "the mouth of the LORD has spoken" and that he spoke "through the mouth of his holy prophets" (e.g., Is 1:20; Acts 3:21 lit.). So out of whose mouth did the prophetic oracles come? The divine mouth or human mouths? The only possible answer is both. God spoke out of his mouth, but through the mouths of the human authors. We must now consider these two truths separately.

First, *the Bible is the Word of God*. The familiar clause in the Apostles' Creed about the Holy Spirit affirms that *he* "spoke through the prophets." They regularly introduced their oracles with the claim that the word of the Lord had come to them. And the apostles made the same claim, even though they did not use the prophetic formulae. The classic statement of the Holy Spirit's work in the inspiration of Scripture remains 2 Timothy 3:16: "All Scripture is given by inspiration of God" (KJV), or literally is God-breathed (*theopneustos*). The word means neither that God breathed into the writers, enabling them to write his word, nor that he breathed into the writings, transforming them from human words into divine words, but rather that what they wrote was breathed out of the mouth of God.[6] This reference to the breath of God is congruous with references elsewhere to his mouth and his words, for in speech our breath communicates our words out of our mouths. It is not literal, of course. Since God is Spirit he has no body, and since he has no body he has neither mouth nor breath. Yet human speech is a readily intelligible model of divine inspiration, since it conveys the thoughts of our minds in words out of our mouth by our breath. It is in this sense that Scripture may accurately be described as 'God-breathed'.

Second, *the Bible is also the words of men*. Some famous Christian leaders have supplemented the model of speech with other models, giving the impression that the process of inspiration was mechanical, and that the human authors played no significant role in it. For example, Tertullian said that the Scriptures were "dictated by the Holy Spirit"; Athenagoras of Athens wrote that "the Spirit used the writers as a flute-player might blow into his flute"; Augustine called them "pens of the Holy Spirit", and Calvin his "amanuenses." But J. I. Packer has shown that these metaphors were used not to define the *process* of inspiration, for which they would have been inappropriate, but to indicate the *result*, namely that Scripture is the Word of God.[7]

The phenomena of Scripture demonstrate quite clearly that the human authors were active and not passive in the process of inspiration. I am referring to the inclusion within the biblical text of history, literature and theology.

1. *Historical narrative.* A substantial amount of both Old Testament and New Testament, in fact approximately a half, consists of narrative— much of the Pentateuch, Joshua, Judges and Ruth, the books of Samuel, Kings and Chronicles, Ezra, Esther and Nehemiah, and in the New Testament the Gospels and the Acts. We do not imagine that the Holy Spirit revealed this history supernaturally; the authors had access to historical documents from which they quoted and which on occasion they incorporated into their text, like the decree of Cyrus the Persian in Ezra 1. Also Luke tells us in the preface to his Gospel about the painstaking investigations in which he had engaged (Lk 1:1-4). So there was no passivity here. Doubtless the Holy Spirit superintended their work, but his inspiration did not make their research unnecessary.

2. *Literary style.* If inspiration had been a mechanical process (the Holy Spirit dictating the biblical text), we would expect to find a uniformity of style and vocabulary. Instead, we find the opposite, an extraordinary diversity of literary genre (narrative, legal code, poetry, prophetic oracle, psalms, proverbs and other wisdom literature, Gospels, letters and apocalypses), of literary styles (ranging from the refined and elegant

to the popular and even vulgar), and of language (each author having his favorite words and phrases). These literary characteristics (genre, style and language) were not ironed out by inspiration.

3. *Theological emphasis.* In the library of sixty-six books that we call the Bible, there is a broad spectrum of theological emphasis, some of which (especially in the Wisdom literature) was evidently the fruit of prolonged reflection. Indeed, it is specifically stated that "the Teacher . . . pondered and searched out and set in order many proverbs" and "searched to find just the right words" (Eccles 12:9-10). Thus, we believe it is not an accident that in the Old Testament Amos was the prophet of God's justice, Hosea of his love, and Isaiah of his sovereignty, or that in the New Testament Paul was the apostle of grace and faith, James of works, John of love, and Peter of hope. The Holy Spirit did not obliterate the individual personality of the human authors any more than their literary style. On the contrary, the Holy Spirit prepared and fashioned the biblical authors (their temperament, genetic inheritance, cultural background, upbringing, education and experience) in such a way as to communicate through each a distinctive and appropriate message. For example, it was through the tragedy of Hosea's broken marriage that God taught Israel about his steadfast covenant love, and through Luke's global horizons as a Gentile and a traveler that God emphasized the universality of the gospel.

Third, *the Bible is the Word of both God and human beings.* We must now bring the two authorships—divine and human—together, and insist on each without thereby contradicting the other.

On the one hand, the Bible is the Word of God. For God spoke through the human authors in such a way as to determine what he intended to say, yet not in such a way as to violate, let alone smother, the personality of the human authors he chose to pen his words. On the other hand, the Bible is the word of men. "Men spoke from God" in such a way as to use their faculties freely, yet not in such a way as to distort, let alone destroy, the message of the divine author. God spoke his words through their words in such a way that their words were simultaneously his. As a result, what they say God says. We have no liberty to declare such a combination impossible. To say so, as Packer states with clarity, indicates

> a false doctrine of God, here particularly of his providence. For it assumes that God and man stand in such a relationship to each other that they cannot both be free agents in the same action. If man acts freely (*i.e.* voluntarily and spontaneously), God does not, and *vice versa*. The two freedoms are mutually exclusive. But the affinities of this idea are with Deism, not Christian Theism.[8]

"The cure for such fallacious reasoning," Packer continues, "is to grasp the biblical idea of God's *concursive operation* in, with and through the free working of man's own mind."[9] In order to clarify this further, various writers (ancient and modern, Roman Catholic and Protestant) have developed an analogy between the two authorships of Scripture and the two natures of Christ.

To be sure, no analogy is perfect, and it is always perilous to argue from an analogy. In this case the imperfection is evident, for the Bible has no *intrinsic* deity as Christ has. Nevertheless, there is in both Christ and Scripture such a combination of the divine and the human that we must affirm each without denying the other. We must preserve each without sacrificing the other. Thus, Jesus is both God and man. We must neither affirm his deity in such a way as to deny the reality of his humanity, nor affirm his humanity in such a way as to deny his deity. Somewhat similarly, the Bible is both divine and human in its authorship. Therefore we must neither affirm its divine origin in such a way as to deny the free activity of the human authors, nor affirm their cooperation in such a way as to deny that through them God spoke his word.

To say that "Jesus is the Son of God" is true, but a dangerous half-truth. It might even be the heresy of docetism (God pretending to be human) unless we add that Jesus is also the Son of Man. To say that "the

Bible is the Word of God" is also true, but a dangerous half-truth. It might even be the heresy of fundamentalism (God dictating mechanically) unless we add that the Bible is the Word of God through words of men. The Bible is equally the Word of God and the word of men. This is the double authorship of the Bible.

The Double Approach to Scripture

The double authorship demands a double approach. Because of the kind of book the Bible is, we must approach it in two distinct yet complementary ways. Because it is the Word of God, we must read it as we would read *no* other book—on our knees, in a humble, reverent, prayerful and submissive frame of mind. But because the Bible is also the word of men, we must read it as we would read *every* other book, thoughtfully and in a "critical" frame of mind. Because we evangelicals tend to neglect the latter, I will take it first.

The "critical" approach to Scripture. The very mention of "biblical criticism" is calculated to send shivers up the average evangelical spine. There are two reasons for this reaction, both of which need to be exorcised.

First, the word *criticism* is often misunderstood. People assume that biblical critics criticize the Bible and pass uniformly negative, even destructive, judgments on it. But *criticism* does not necessarily have this meaning. For example, a literary critic is not someone who criticizes literature and finds fault with everything he reads but a scholar who reviews and assesses books. It is the same with an art or drama critic. Similarly, a biblical critic is not necessarily someone determined to discredit the biblical documents but a scholar who examines and evaluates them from different points of view. In these spheres, *criticism* means not destruction but investigation, not judgment but evaluation.

The second reason for our evangelical suspicion of biblical criticism is that the first critics about 250 years ago were extremely skeptical scholars, products of the so-called Age of Reason or European Enlightenment. They were rationalistic and unbelieving in their approach to

Scripture and consistently destructive in their conclusions.

One of the earliest and worst offenders was the eighteenth-century deist Hermann Reimarus, professor of Oriental languages in the University of Hamburg. He was outspoken in his rejection of revelation, miracles, and the deity, atoning death and resurrection of Jesus. He also drew attention, almost with glee, to the discrepancies which he believed were to be found in the resurrection narratives. He and others like him gave biblical criticism a bad name.

But just as *criticism* does not necessarily mean "judgment," so its practitioners ("biblical critics") are not necessarily all unbelievers. Many are devout and reverent believers. Greatly to oversimplify a complex subject, we may say that there are four main types of biblical criticism.

First, there is *textual* criticism, whose admirable goal is to establish the authentic text of Scripture.

Second, there is *historical* criticism, which is concerned both to study the historical circumstances in which the biblical books were composed and to evaluate the historical element in the text itself.

Third, *literary* criticism examines both the sources which the author had at his disposal and the forms in which oral material was preserved and made available to them.

The fourth, *redaction criticism*, is valuable because it recognizes that the biblical authors and editors (redactors) had a theological motivation behind their writing.

By using these critical tools in our study, we are acknowledging the human aspects (literary, historical and theological) of the biblical text. In all four kinds of biblical criticism the most important question concerns the presuppositions with which the critic approaches the text: are they Christian or sub-Christian? His conclusions will be determined largely by this. The three most common sub-Christian presuppositions, which have led to disastrous conclusions, are as follows:

1. History is a closed continuum of cause and effect, with no possibility

of divine intervention or prophecy.

2. The universe is a self-contained system, in which miracles are impossible.

3. Religion is a human phenomenon, which has evolved over the centuries from primitive animism through polytheism to monotheism. There is no such thing as revelation.

These presuppositions are not Christian. They reflect a thoroughgoing skepticism which is incompatible with biblical faith. Those who hold them will come into continuous collision with the Bible and with its very different understanding of history, cosmology and religion.

The "reverent" approach to Scripture. Having considered the "critical" approach to Scripture, we come now to the "reverent" approach. They complement and do not exclude or contradict one another, for in the critical approach we scrutinize Scripture, while in the reverent approach we invite Scripture to scrutinize us.

Because we believe that Scripture is "God's Word written" (*Anglican Article* 20), it is unlike every other book. We therefore approach it as we approach no other book. We kneel—not because we worship the Bible but because we worship the God of the Bible and desire to humble ourselves before him. We remember the words of Jesus that God actively hides himself from some (the arrogant), while revealing himself to babies (NIV "little children," Mt 11:25), that is, those who are humble in their approach. So we sit at our Master's feet, like Mary of Bethany, listening to his words (Lk 10:39). We pray like the boy Samuel, "Speak, for your servant is listening" (1 Sam 3:10). We cry to the Holy Spirit, who is the divine author of the book, to be its interpreter also, and to illumine our darkened minds. We ask God to break through our defenses, until we are ready to hear not the soothing echoes of our own cultural prejudice but the thunderclap of his Word.

I fear this risky humility before God is tragically absent in many biblical critics, and also in some evangelical preachers. Just as, for a true and balanced understanding of Scripture, we must combine its divine and human elements and see it as God's Word through the human authors, so also, for a true and balanced approach to Scripture, we must combine the critical and the reverent, and come to it with both diligent study and earnest prayer. I conclude this section with two examples, one from the Old Testament and the other from the New.

When Daniel was granted a vision beside the River Tigris, the heavenly being who appeared said to him: "Do not be afraid, Daniel. Since the first day that you set your mind to gain understanding and to humble yourself before your God, your words were heard, and I have come in response to them" (Dan 10:12). Similarly, when Paul was anxious that Timothy would understand and obey the instructions he was giving him, he urged him to combine his own reflection with dependence on the Lord for illumination, that is, study and prayer. "Reflect on what I am saying, for the Lord will give you insight into all this" (2 Tim 2:7).

AUTHORITY

If the word *revelation* emphasizes God's initiative in making himself known, and *inspiration* denotes the process he employed, then *authority* indicates the result. Because Scripture is the revelation of God by the inspiration of the Spirit, it has authority over us. But our day detests authority. We are searching for freedom, and it is everywhere assumed (though falsely) that all authority will inhibit our quest, indeed that authority and freedom are incompatible. Ever since the 1960s, when the Free Speech movement erupted at the University of California, Berkeley, and the students took to the barricades on the streets of Paris, a strong antiauthority mood has prevailed. Every authority figure and every established institution is called into question. A "radical" is precisely somebody who refuses to accept anything merely because it is laid down from on high or inherited from the past.

Moreover, this revolt against authority in the world has been accompanied by a loss of authority in the church. Consider the multiplicity of

Protestant denominations and our tendency to go on splintering; the competing factions in the ancient churches of the East and the West, as cracks appear in those mighty monoliths; the controversies in and about the World Council of Churches, whose doctrinal basis is good but minimal; and the unedifying spectacle on television of church leaders either not knowing what they believe or, if they do, then disagreeing with one another about it. It is a state of theological confusion, even chaos. And its basic cause is the lack of agreement on how to agree, that is, on the question of authority.

In theory, all Christians confess that "Jesus Christ is Lord" (e.g., Phil 2:9-11), for after his resurrection he claimed that "all authority in heaven and on earth" had been delegated to him (Mt 28:18). The whole New Testament takes it for granted that the church is under the authority of the risen Lord Jesus. Charles Lamb, the nineteenth-century British essayist, is reputed to have said, "If Shakespeare were to enter this room, we would rise with respect to greet him; but if [Jesus] were to come in, we would fall down and try to kiss the hem of his garment."

For myself I think we would do more than kiss his clothing; we would confess with Thomas, "My Lord and my God!" If Jesus Christ were to appear visibly in such a way that no one would question his identity, and if he were to speak audibly in such a way that no one would mistake his meaning, it is charitable to suppose that the church would listen, believe and obey. But Jesus Christ will not appear like that and address his church, at least not until he comes on the last day, and then it will be too late.

So how does the Lord Jesus exercise his authority and govern his church today? Four main answers have been given to this question.

1. The *Roman Catholic* answer is that Christ rules his church through the *magisterium*, the teaching authority given to the Pope and his college of bishops both in the present and through past tradition. The Orthodox churches also stress tradition, especially through the first seven ecumenical councils.

2. The *liberal* answer is that Christ rules his church through the indi-

vidual reason and conscience, illumined by the Holy Spirit, or through the consensus of educated opinion. They sometimes add experience to reason, wanting to unite the rational with the emotional, and the authority of experience is stressed by Pentecostal and charismatic Christians too.

3. A popular *Anglican* answer is that Christ rules his church through the "threefold cord" of Scripture, tradition and reason. In other words, authority is dispersed, not centralized. It is typical of the "sweet reasonableness" of Anglicanism to avoid polarizations and opt for a *via media*. But in practice the threefold cord is unworkable. For what happens if and when the three authorities are in conflict with one another? Then Scripture must take precedence. Richard Hooker, to whose *Ecclesiastical Polity* (1593-1597) Anglican leaders often appeal, did not in fact teach that Scripture, tradition and reason are equal authorities. Hooker wrote:

> What Scripture doth plainly deliver, to that the *first* place both of credit and obedience is due; the *next* whereunto is whatsoever any man can necessarily conclude by force of reason; *after these* the voice of the Church succeedeth.[10]

4. The *evangelical* answer is that Christ rules his church through Scripture. Scripture is the scepter by which King Jesus reigns. Tradition is important, for it includes the teaching of the early councils and the creeds. We evangelicals should develop a deeper respect for tradition, since it is the church's interpretation of Scripture down the ages, as the Holy Spirit has enlightened it. Not of course that all tradition correctly interprets Scripture. But to ignore it altogether is to behave as if we thought the Holy Spirit began his teaching ministry, and even came into existence, only when we appeared on the scene! Nevertheless, Jesus himself subordinated tradition to Scripture, calling the former "the traditions of men" and the latter "the word of God" (Mk 7:1-13). We must do the same, assigning to tradition a secondary place, including the traditions of the evangelical elders. Reason and experience are also important, for God has made us both rational and emotional creatures. But the

proper place of reason is not to stand in judgment upon Scripture, but instead to sit in humility under it, seeking to elucidate and apply it; and the experience of the burning heart is a major way by which the Holy Spirit attests the truth of his Word (Lk 24:32).

There is one particular promise of Christ which these four groups—Roman Catholics, liberals, Anglicans and evangelicals—all claim for themselves! It is his promise that, when the Holy Spirit has come, the Spirit of truth, "he will guide you into all truth" (Jn 16:12-13). Roman Catholics apply it to their bishops as the supposed successors of the apostles. Liberals insist that it is the individual whom the Spirit leads into the truth, or the contemporary church. A brash statement to this effect was recently made by Frank Griswold, presiding bishop of the American Episcopal Church. The Episcopal Church has certainly gone beyond Scripture, he conceded. How is this justified? "Jesus talked about the Spirit guiding the church into all truth." C. E. Bennison, bishop of Pennsylvania, has gone even further. "Because we wrote the Bible," he has said with bland self-confidence, "we can re-write it." But we did not write the Bible. In the New Testament letters, for example, the church was not writing in its own name. On the contrary, the apostles addressed the church in the name of Christ.

Let us return to Christ's promise that the Spirit of truth will lead "you" into all the truth. Who is this "you"? It is a crucial hermeneutical question. I venture to say that both Catholics and liberals are wrong, for the "you" cannot possibly refer to them. It refers rather to the apostles.

Consider the context. Jesus said, "I have much more to say to *you*, more than *you* can now bear. But when he, the Spirit of truth, comes, he will guide *you* into all truth . . . he will tell *you* what is yet to come" (Jn 16:12-13). The first two *yous* unquestionably refer to the apostles, who during the earthly ministry of Jesus were unable to assimilate all he had to teach them. So the third and fourth *you* must refer to them too. We cannot change the identity of the *you* in the middle of the sentence. What Jesus promised was that the Spirit of truth would accomplish after Pentecost what Jesus had not been able to accomplish during his public ministry. The promise was fulfilled in the writing of the New Testament.

The reason the church has historically submitted to Scripture, and why evangelicals continue to do so, is that our Lord Jesus himself did. Thus the authority of Christ and the authority of Scripture belong together. The church has no liberty to repudiate what her Lord has affirmed. Of course Jesus lived between the two Testaments. He looked back to the Old Testament, which was already complete, and he looked forward to the New Testament, which had not yet begun. So the way in which he affirmed them was necessarily different. He confirmed the authority of the Old Testament by endorsing it. He obeyed its moral commands, responding to temptation with a firm *gegraptai gar* ("because it stands written"); he accepted its teaching about his messianic mission as the Son of Man and the servant of the Lord ("The Son of Man must suffer"); and in his public debates with both Pharisees and Sadducees he made Scripture the final court of appeal ("This is why you are wrong, that you don't know the Scriptures"). His own attitude of humble submission to Scripture is incontrovertible; and it is inconceivable that his disciples should have a lower view of it than their Master.[11]

The case for the authority of the New Testament is different. The argument now is that Jesus not only foresaw the writing of New Testament Scripture, parallel to the Old Testament, but intended it for the same reason (to record and interpret what God was doing). So Jesus made provision for it by appointing and equipping his twelve apostles. Their threefold uniqueness lay in their personal authorization by Jesus, their eyewitness experience of him (Paul being added as a witness to the resurrection) and their extraordinary inspiration by the Holy Spirit. In consequence, they spoke and wrote in the name of Christ with the self-conscious authority of his apostles. Paul even thanked God for the Galatians in these terms: "You welcomed me as if I were an angel of God, as if I were Christ Jesus himself" (Gal 4:14).

I am thankful that the Anglican bishops, gathered for their Lambeth

Conference in 1958, stated that the New Testament books "were recognised as giving the witness of the apostles to the life, teaching, death and resurrection of the Lord and the interpretation by the apostles of these events. To that apostolic authority the church must ever bow."[12] So then our Lord Jesus Christ repeatedly endorsed the authority of the Old Testament by appealing to it and submitting to it. He also deliberately provided for the writing of the New Testament by appointing and equipping his apostles. In this way both the Old Testament and the New Testament, although in different ways, bear the stamp of his authority. Therefore, if we wish to submit to the authority of Christ, we must submit to the authority of Scripture, since the authority of Scripture carries with it the authority of Christ.

THREE MORE WORDS

We have concentrated so far, for our understanding of Scripture, on the three words *revelation, inspiration* and *authority,* although with the addition of *supremacy* to indicate that the authority of Scripture is supreme over lesser authorities like tradition, reason and experience. Now, for the sake of completeness, we need to consider three more words, which also belong to the evangelical view of the Bible.

Perspicuity

The perspicuity of Scripture was much insisted on by the Reformers. They meant that it has a "perspicuous," "see-through" or transparent quality. They did not mean by this that everything in Scripture is plain. How could they, when the Ethiopian confessed his need of a teacher to explain things to him (Acts 8:31) and when Peter confessed that Paul's letters contained "some things that are hard to understand" (2 Pet 3:16)? If one apostle could not always understand another apostle, it would hardly be modest for us to claim that we can!

No, the Reformers' insistence was that the essence of the biblical message, the way of salvation in Christ by grace through faith, is simple enough for even the uneducated to grasp. Hence their determination to put a vernacular Bible into the hands of laypeople. The perspicuity of Scripture was well defined in the Westminster Confession (1643-1646):

> All things in Scripture are not alike plain in themselves, nor alike clear unto all; yet those things which are necessary to be known, believed and observed for salvation, are so clearly propounded and opened in some place of Scripture or another, that not only the learned but the unlearned, in a due use of the ordinary means, may attain unto a sufficient understanding of them. (1.7)

Sufficiency

The sufficiency of Scripture (*sola Scriptura*) was another Reformation concern. The Reformers did not mean by it that Scripture is sufficient for education, but that it is sufficient for salvation. They did not suppose that Christians should read nothing but the Bible. Following the invention of printing, they encouraged people to educate themselves, to read other books, and to develop a broad culture. But for salvation only one book was necessary.

The sufficiency of Scripture is due to the sufficiency of Christ to whom it witnesses. *Anglican Article* 6 puts the matter succinctly:

> Holy Scripture containeth all things necessary to salvation: so that whatsoever is not read therein, nor may be proved thereby, is not to be required of any man, that it should be believed as an article of the Faith, or be thought requisite or necessary to salvation.

The article was framed with the Church of Rome in mind, since it required (and still requires) its members to accept a number of traditions with no biblical warrant. Today the challenge comes rather from some Pentecostal and charismatic church leaders who claim that God is again giving apostles and prophets to his church, and that their teaching supplements Scripture. All evangelicals will want to agree that there are today both apostolic ministries (e.g., pioneer missionaries, church planters and church leaders including bishops) and prophetic ministries (e.g., in addressing specific situations with wisdom from God). But evangelicals should also be able to agree that there are no apostles or prophets today who have an authority comparable to that of the biblical apostles and prophets, whose teaching is the foundation of the church (Eph 2:20). If there were, their teaching would need to be added to Scripture and the principle of its sufficiency would have been breached.

Inerrancy

Since the publication in 1976 of Harold Lindsell's book *Battle for the Bible*, the battle among American evangelicals has really been over the word *inerrancy*, whose equivalent in British debate has been *infallibility*. There are at least five reasons why the word *inerrancy* makes me uncomfortable.

First, God's self-revelation in Scripture is so rich—both in content and in form—that it cannot be reduced to a string of propositions which invites the label *truth* or *error*. "True or false?" would be an inappropriate question to address to a great deal of Scripture.

Second, the word *inerrancy* is a double negative, and I always prefer a single positive to a double negative. It is better to affirm that the Bible is true and therefore trustworthy. J. I. Packer clarifies in his lectures that what inerrantists are essentially concerned about is "total trustworthiness as a consequence of entire truthfulness."[13] And with that all evangelicals would (or should) agree.

Third, the word *inerrancy* sends out the wrong signals and develops the wrong attitudes. Instead of encouraging us to search the Scriptures so that we may grow in grace and in the knowledge of God, it seems to turn us into detectives hunting for incriminating clues and to make us excessively defensive in relation to apparent discrepancies.

Fourth, it is unwise and unfair to use *inerrancy* as a shibboleth by which to identify who is evangelical and who is not. The hallmark of authentic evangelicalism is not subscription but submission. That is, it is not whether we subscribe to an impeccable formula about the Bible but whether we live in practical submission to what the Bible teaches, including an advance resolve to submit to whatever it may later be shown to teach.

Fifth, it is impossible to prove that the Bible contains no errors. When faced with an apparent discrepancy, the most Christian response is neither to make a premature negative judgment nor to resort to a contrived harmonization but rather to suspend judgment, waiting patiently for further illumination to be given us. Many former problems have been solved in this way.

When some 650 American evangelical leaders gathered in 1989 for a consultation on "evangelical affirmations," cosponsored by the National Association of Evangelicals and Trinity Evangelical Divinity School, they issued a fine, comprehensive statement. Here is part of their affirmation about the Bible:

> We affirm the complete truthfulness and the full and final authority of the Old and New Testament Scriptures as the Word of God written. The appropriate response to it is humble assent and obedience.

Then, as part of their conclusion they wrote:

> Evangelicals hold the Bible to be God's Word and therefore completely true and trustworthy (and this is what we mean by the words *infallible* and *inerrant*).[14]

TWO CLARIFICATIONS

When evangelicals affirm that Scripture is God's Word, they have two vital clarifications in mind.

First, they are referring to Scripture *as originally given*. For example, the International Fellowship of Evangelical Students (IFES) affirms the inspiration of Scripture in its doctrinal basis "as originally given." We do not claim authority for any particular text or translation but only for the original text as it was written down by its author.

Our critics begin at this point to smile and snigger, because of course all the biblical autographs have been lost. What is the point, they ask, of assigning authority to a text which does not exist? But we evangelicals are ready to face our critics' mockery, for this first qualification is very important to us. We know that the Hebrew and Greek manuscripts which have come down to us, even the great codices of the fourth century A.D., contain some copyists' errors. But we do not claim divine inspiration for their mistakes! On the contrary, evangelicals are committed (as we have already noted) to the science of textual criticism, which compares manuscripts, versions (translations) and citations (quotations by the church fathers) with a view to establishing the original text. This remains one of the church's vital responsibilities.

Second, we are referring to Scripture *as correctly interpreted.* Just as we do not claim divine authority for copyists' mistakes, so we do not claim divine authority for interpreters' mistakes. Moreover, in seeking to discover the true interpretation of a text, the most important principle concerns the intention of its author: "A text means what its author meant."[15] Therefore, to "banish the original author as the determiner of meaning" is to "reject the only compelling normative principle that could lend validity to an interpretation."[16]

Postmodernists, however, "deconstruct" texts, that is, detach them from their authors and expect their readers to determine their meaning as they wish. Evangelicals must not surrender to this novel and disastrous deconstructionism. We prefer the Lausanne Covenant, which describes Scripture as "without error in all that it affirms."[17] This qualifying clause is essential. Just as the words "as originally given" commit us to the discipline of textual criticism, so the words "in all that it affirms" and "as correctly interpreted" commit us to the discipline of hermeneutics. Two examples may be helpful.

First, we must not imagine that all Old Testament characters are presented to us as good examples to be imitated, for some set a bad example which is rather to be avoided (see 1 Cor 10:1-11). In some passages we are told explicitly whether a story is recorded as a "warning" for us (1 Cor 10:11) or as an "encouragement" (Rom 15:4). At other times no moral judgment is passed, and we are left to make up our own minds in the light of the rest of Scripture. In a third kind of narrative we are given both positive and negative signals simultaneously, not least during that dark age presided over by the judges. True, Samson and Jephthah are celebrated among the heroes of faith in Hebrews 11:32, since they were loyal to Yahweh even when surrounded by Baal worship. But some of their conduct was deplorable. Samson behaved like a mixed-up, overgrown adolescent without self-control, and Jephthah should definitely not have sacrificed his daughter to his vow, since human sacrifice was one of the main evils for which God had said that the land would "vomit out" its inhabitants. Although the writer does not clearly condemn the prevailing morals, he hints at his disapproval by his repeated refrain that "in those days Israel had no king; everyone did as he saw fit" (Judg 17:6; 21:25; cf. Judg 18:1; 19:1).

A second question concerns the Gospels. We must not impose on them our standards of computer accuracy, and expect them to conform to it. Chronology is an example. Matthew and Mark both place Jesus' visit to Nazareth (together with his synagogue sermon and his rejection by his own people) in the middle of his public ministry. But Luke places it at the very beginning, immediately after his baptism and temptations (Lk 4:14ff.). There is no need, however, to accuse Luke of error. He evidently sees the Nazareth incident as forecasting Jesus' ministry and rejection. So he puts it at the beginning as a kind of signpost, deliberately presenting his chronology to make a theological point. We must allow every biblical author to lay down his own theological emphases and literary principles, and to abide by them.

Here then are the two important clarifications. While affirming the entire truthfulness and trustworthiness of Scripture, we are referring to Scripture (a) as originally given and (b) as correctly interpreted. It will mean more work for us as we labor to interpret and apply Scripture accurately, and it will remove from us some of the easy certainties which our critics suggest we are longing for. But it will enable us to guard our integrity, for although we sometimes disagree on our interpretations, the biblical text itself remains normative, and we have the permanent duty and right to keep returning to it, to keep scrutinizing all interpretations in the light of it, and to keep revising them accordingly.

I hope that this rather long chapter has demonstrated that we evangelical people are first and foremost Bible people, affirming the great truths of revelation, inspiration and authority. We have a higher view of Scripture than anybody else in the church. Our use of it should therefore correspond to our view of it.

Like everybody else, Bible people are busy people, and there is never enough time to do everything we ought or want to do. Nevertheless, we must struggle to make time every day for some personal Bible reading, since our spiritual life, health and growth are nurtured by it. And although family prayers at the breakfast table may nowadays be impossible for most, with the adults dashing to work and the children to school, yet a Christian family should be able to manage a little time together around the Bible every week, perhaps on Saturday or Sunday.

As for the church, if we are pastors, I hope we will recommit ourselves to the wholesome discipline of biblical preaching, and if we are lay people encourage our pastors to do so. The conscientious exposition of the Word of God from the pulpit remains an essential characteristic of evangelical churches. The words of Jesus, quoting Deuteronomy, still come to us across the centuries, that human beings do not live by bread only, but by every word that comes from the mouth of God (e.g., Mk 4:4).

SUGGESTED FURTHER READING

Boice, James Montgomery. *Foundations of the Christian Faith.* Downers Grove, Ill.: InterVarsity Press, 1996.

Fee, Gordon, and Douglas Stuart. *How to Read the Bible for All Its Worth.*

Grand Rapids: Zondervan, 1993.

Sproul, R. C. *The Holiness of God*. Rev. ed. Wheaton, Ill.: Tyndale House, 1998.

————. *Knowing Scripture*. Downers Grove, Ill.: InterVarsity Press, 1977.

Sterrett, T. Norton. *How to Understand Your Bible*. Downers Grove, Ill.: InterVarsity Press, 1974.

2

The Cross of Christ

IF THE FIRST ESSENTIAL OF EVANGELICAL CHRISTIANITY is the revelation of God in the Bible, the second is the cross of Christ, together with all the glorious benefits he achieved by it.

I invite you to reflect with me in this chapter on one of the most extraordinary statements which the apostle Paul ever made—which is to claim a great deal, since he made a good many astonishing statements. The one I am referring to is Galatians 6:14 (REB):

> God forbid that I should boast of anything but the cross of our Lord Jesus Christ, through which the world is crucified to me and I to the world!

There is no exact equivalent in English, or I believe in many other languages, to the Greek verb *kauchaomai*. It may be translated "to boast in," "to glory in," "to take pride in," "to revel in," even "to live for." In a word, our *kauchēma* is our obsession. It engrosses our attention, it fills our horizons, it dominates our mind. For Paul this was the cross. The cross of Christ was the center of his faith, of his life and of his ministry; it should equally be the center of ours. Let others be obsessed with money, success, fame, sex or power; those who follow Christ should be obsessed with him and with his cross.

This was not, however, a peculiarity of Paul's. On the contrary, the cross was central to his mind because it had been central to the mind of Christ. Did Jesus not repeatedly predict the necessity of his suffering, saying that "the Son of man must suffer many things and be rejected . . . and be killed" (Mk 8:31; cf. Mk 9:12, 31; 10:34, 45)? Did he not speak of his death as the "hour" for which he had come into the world (e.g., Jn 12:23, 27)? Did he not give instructions for his own memorial service, telling his disciples to eat bread and drink wine in memory of him? Further, since he called the bread his body "given" for them, and the wine his blood "shed" for them, it is evident that he intended death, not life, to speak from both the elements. It was therefore by his death that he wished above all to be remembered.

So the church was right in its choice of symbol for Christianity. There were many options. It could have chosen the crib in which the baby Jesus was cradled (emblem of the incarnation), or the carpenter's bench at which he worked in Nazareth (emblem of the dignity of manual labor), or the boat on the lake of Galilee which he used as a pulpit (emblem of his teaching ministry), or the towel which he tied round him when he washed and wiped his disciples' feet (emblem of humble servitude), or the tomb in which his body was laid and from which he rose (emblem of his resurrection), or the throne which he occupies today at the Father's right hand (emblem of his supreme sovereignty), or the dove, the wind or the fire (emblems of the Holy Spirit). Any one of these could have been an appropriate symbol for the religion of Jesus Christ.

But the church passed them by and chose the cross instead. We see it everywhere—in the great cathedrals of medieval Europe, whose nave and chancel deliberately display a cruciform ground plan, on the necklaces of Christian women and on the lapels of Christian men. For the Christian faith is the faith of Christ crucified. In this faith we were baptized, and in some traditions signed with the sign of the cross, traced with water on our forehead. In this faith we are called to live, to serve and to die, and after our death our family and friends may well erect a cross over our grave. Of course we must never separate the crucifixion from the incarnation and the resurrection of Jesus. His death would have had no efficacy if it had not been preceded by his unique birth and followed by his unique resurrection. Only the God-man could die for our sins, and only the resurrection could validate his death. Paul notably bears witness to this by bringing the three great events together. "There is one God," he wrote to Timothy, "and one mediator between God and men, the man Christ Jesus, who gave himself as a ransom for all" (1 Tim 2:5-6). In this one short sentence Jesus is named "mediator," "man" and "ransom," for he was incarnate as man, he died as a ransom, and he has been exalted as our heavenly mediator. The three are linked together inextricably.

Nevertheless, although none is effective without the others, it is the death which is central. For the birth looks forward to it and prepares for it, while the resurrection looks back to it and validates it. Consider some of the great apostolic pronouncements about the death of Jesus Christ:

While we were still sinners, Christ died for us. (Rom 5:8)

Christ died for our sins. (1 Cor 15:3)

[He] gave himself for our sins. (Gal 1:4)

In him we have redemption through his blood, the forgiveness of sins. (Eph 1:7)

Since we have confidence to enter the Most Holy Place by the blood of Jesus . . . let us draw near to God. (Heb 10:19-22)

Christ died for sins once for all, the righteous for the unrighteous, to bring you to God. (1 Pet 3:18)

God . . . loved us and sent his Son as an atoning sacrifice for our sins. (1 Jn 4:10)

You are worthy . . . because you were slain, and with your blood you purchased men for God. (Rev 5:9)

This is only a selection of texts. But here the principal writers of the New Testament (Paul, Peter, John, the writer to the Hebrews and the author of the Revelation) all bear witness to the same central truth: it was by the shedding of his blood, that is, by his sacrificial and violent death on the cross, that Jesus dealt with our sins and won our salvation.

Moreover, the centrality of the cross has been widely recognized during the last hundred years or so. I share a few striking statements with my readers. Here is J. C. Ryle, the great evangelical bishop of Liverpool from 1880 to 1900:

> If you have not yet found out that Christ crucified is the foundation of the whole volume, you have read your Bible hitherto to very little profit. Your religion is a heaven without a sun, an arch without a keystone, a compass without a needle, a clock without spring or weights, a lamp without oil. . . . Beware, I say again, of a religion without the cross.[1]

P. T. Forsyth, a Congregationalist theologian who died in 1921, wrote three perceptive books on the cross. Here are two quotations—a statement and a warning:

> Christ is to us just what his cross is. All that Christ was in heaven or on earth was put into what he did there. . . . You do not understand Christ till you understand his cross.[2]

> On this interpretation of the work of Christ [Paul's doctrine of reconciliation] the whole church rests. If you move faith from that centre, you have driven the nail into the church's coffin. The church is then doomed to death, and it is only a matter of time when she shall expire.[3]

We owe much to Leon Morris of Melbourne, Australia, for his three or four characteristically comprehensive books on different aspects of the cross. In one he gave his carefully considered opinion: "The cross dominates the New Testament."[4]

But why is the cross central? In particular, why did Paul glory only in the cross? In the Greco-Roman world of the first century the cross was regarded as an object of distaste, even of disgust. How could Paul glory in this symbol of shame? Can we elaborate what he meant? Yes, we can. It is a basic hermeneutical principle that we must allow the context to determine the meaning of the text. And since Galatians 6:14 belongs to the conclusion of his letter to the Galatians, the rest of it, and specially its references to the cross, will help us to understand Paul's meaning.

OUR ACCEPTANCE WITH GOD

First, we glory in the cross for our acceptance with God. Indeed, there is no other way of acceptance with him. Some years ago, when I was in Durham, in the north of England, I worshiped on Sunday morning in the massive Norman cathedral which dominates the city and university. The preacher during that service was H. E. W. Turner, a well-known New Testament scholar at that time. I was arrested when in the middle of his sermon he asked himself a personal question. (It is not the custom in Britain for university professors to ask themselves embarrassing questions in public!) "How can I, a lost and guilty sinner, stand before a just and holy God?" Good question! It is arguably the most important of all questions which confront human beings.

If we have never asked ourselves this question, we must be very short-sighted indeed, for one thing is certain: we can never enter the holy presence of God, either in this life or in the next, in the tattered rags of our own morality. We are unfit even to approach him. All those who have been granted even a momentary glimpse of his majesty have not been able to bear the sight. They have either shrunk from him in shame like Moses at the burning bush (Ex 3:6) or fallen prostrate at his feet like Ezekiel in the Old Testament and John in the New (Ezek 1:28; Rev 1:17). If we were to penetrate his presence, unbidden and unprepared, we would shrivel up and be consumed.

This sense of our sinfulness, of the blinding holiness of God, and of the absolute incompatibility of the one with the other, is an essential evangelical characteristic, without which our understanding of the necessity and the nature of the cross is bound to be skewed. It is why Bishop Ryle gave as the second leading feature of evangelical religion (the first being the supremacy of Scripture) "the depth and prominence it assigns to the doctrine of human sinfulness and corruption." "We hold," he continued, "that a mighty spiritual disease like this requires a mighty spiritual medicine for its cure."[5]

Yet it is precisely here that our detractors criticize us. In 1945 Geoffrey Fisher, archbishop of Canterbury, commissioned a group of Anglican Catholics to examine the causes of Catholic-Protestant deadlock and to consider whether synthesis, or at least coexistence, might be possible. Two years later their report *Catholicity* was published.[6] They accused evangelicals of "grievous distortion," "radical error" and "a catastrophic pessimism concerning the results of the Fall, formulated in the doctrine of man's 'total depravity,' and the complete destruction of the *imago Dei* in human nature."[7] It was an extraordinarily inept and inaccurate criticism, however, as a group of Anglican evangelicals commissioned by Geoffrey Fisher in 1947 had no difficulty in showing. It is true, they agreed, that "by sin man's whole nature is perverted, and infected with self-will and self-love," but the divine image in us, though defaced, has certainly not been destroyed (see Gen 9:6; Jas 3:9). Further, " 'total depravity' means not that there is no good in man but that even his best acts and characteristics are subtly and deeply tainted with pride."[8] Evangelicals insist on this, and one hopes that Catholics do too.

This debate is of the utmost importance. I will not mince my words. To make light of sin is inevitably to make light of salvation and so of the cross. To deny the just judgment of God is a characteristic of false prophets, "who say 'peace, peace' when there is no peace." They are like bad builders whose remedy for a flimsy wall about to collapse is to apply a coat of whitewash. They are like bad doctors who dress a deep wound superficially, as though it were not serious (see Jer 6:14; 8:11; Ezek 13:10ff.).

But our human condition without Christ is extremely serious. We are "lost and guilty sinners," as Turner rightly said. This is why we set ourselves resolutely against the human potential movement, which has become so widespread and done such damage, especially in the United States. It accuses us of a morbid obsession with guilt. In fact, it deplores all mention of sin, guilt, judgment, atonement and repentance as inimical to our mental and spiritual health. It then tries to reinterpret salvation in terms of a recovery of our self-esteem.

In response, although we acknowledge that there are such things as false guilt and inferiority feelings, and although we should never attempt to induce these in people artificially, yet guilt for objective wrongdoing must be acknowledged as a reality, and confessed. Otherwise we will never flee to Christ crucified for forgiveness and a new start. To wallow in guilt is pathological; to cry to God for mercy is the beginning of health.

Do not let us be deceived, then, by those false teachers who minimize the sinfulness of sin. Biography and autobiography often reveal unsuspected corruption beneath the surface of respectability. Many historical examples could be given. I content myself with two.

The first is Dag Hammarskjöld, Secretary-General of the United Nations, a deeply committed public servant, described by W. H. Auden as "a great, good and lovable man." But he had a very different opinion of himself. He bemoaned what he called "that dark counter-centre of evil in our nature," and in particular the perversity which "makes our unselfish service of others the foundation of our own self-esteem."[9]

My second example is Cyril Garbett, who was archbishop of York from 1942 to 1955. Writing in his diary on his eightieth birthday, he felt the need to distinguish between the public *persona* and the private reality:

> People have been undeservedly kind, they have formed an ideal picture of myself—the devoted pastor, the kindly old gentleman, and the courageous prophet!! They don't see me as I really am, selfish, self-centred, seeking and enjoying the praise of men, lazy, possessive, and timid.[10]

Which of us, if given the chance to write an autobiography, would not express the same paradox? Sin is self, and Luther was on target when he described fallen and unregenerate man as *homo in se incurvatus* ("man curved in on himself"). In his lectures on Romans, he wrote that "our nature has been so deeply curved in upon itself" that "it even uses God himself to achieve" its own ends. Again, "this curved-ness is now natural for us."[11] Swiss theologian Emil Brunner was not exaggerating when he dubbed "a superficial person" anybody who "has not yet perceived that evil is entwined with the very roots of his personality."[12] As Jesus said, it comes out of the heart (Mk 7:20-23).

Not yet, however, have we plumbed the depths of human evil. There is worse to come. It is not just that our fallen nature is crookedly bent, twisted, self-absorbed and self-obsessed. It is also, as perceptive theologians like Brunner have observed, that we have risen up in active rebellion against a holy God. We have certainly not loved him with all our being. Instead, as Brunner wrote in his Christian anthropology *Man in Revolt*, we have been guilty of "defiance, arrogance, the desire to be equal with God."[13]

Even more outspoken was Brunner's definition of sin:

> Sin is the desire for the autonomy of man; therefore, in the last resort, it is the denial of God and self-deification: it is getting rid of the Lord God, and the proclamation of self-sovereignty.[14]

When sin is stripped of all its disguises and is seen in its ugly nakedness as the attempt to dethrone God and enthrone self, it is evident that we are incapable of doing anything to gain acceptance with God. To be sure, the ethnic religions assure us with one voice that it is perfectly possible to do so, to accumulate merit, and to commend ourselves to God. For example, in a lecture during the first Parliament of Religions in Chicago in 1893, Swami Vivekananda, the Hindu reformer and founder of the Ramakrishna Mission, said:

> The Hindu refuses to call you sinners. Ye are the children of God; the sharers of immortal bliss, holy and perfect beings. Ye divinities on earth,

sinners? It is a sin to call a man a sinner. It is a standing libel on human nature.[15]

In another essay he wrote, "Silly fools tell you, you are sinners. . . . You are all God."[16]

So there is the stark alternative. Either we are God or we are rebels against God. Only the Bible, of all the world's holy books, insists not just that we are sinners but that in consequence we are under the judgment of God, that self-salvation is impossible and that our only hope is in the cross.

At last now, after this long but necessary excursus on the reality and horror of sin, we are ready to return to Galatians, and to the cross as the only way of acceptance with God:

> Christ redeemed us from the curse of the law by becoming a curse for us, for it is written: "Cursed is everyone who is hung on a tree." (Gal 3:13)

These words have been described as "startling, almost shocking." They declare that the only way by which we can be redeemed from the curse of the law (that is, from the judgment which God's law pronounces on those who disobey it) is that Christ bore it in our place; that he became a curse instead of us; that he endured in his own innocent person the condemnation we had deserved. This is called "penal substitution." J. I. Packer has justly called it "a distinguishing mark of the world-wide evangelical fraternity."[17] Only because Christ bore the curse can we inherit the blessing (Gal 3:6-14).

Of course we must protect this doctrine from misunderstanding and hedge it with every possible safeguard. We must never suggest, for example, that God the Father was reluctant to come to our rescue, and that Jesus Christ was a third party who intervened between God and us. No, no! It was God himself who took the initiative in his holy love for us. "God was in Christ reconciling the world to himself" (2 Cor 5:19 REB). Yet what God did in and through Christ was to take our place, to bear our sin, to endure our curse, and to die our death, so that we might be forgiven. Moreover, the Christian life continues where it begins, at the foot of the cross of Jesus. The cross is not an elementary stage which we later grow out of. We never graduate from the school of Calvary. And the Lord's Supper continuously brings us back to it.

For several pages now we have been reflecting on human depravity and the centrality of the cross. We are hell-deserving sinners. The expression is archaic but accurate. Do we really think that in ourselves we are fit to be admitted into God's holy presence? Of course not! The very idea is preposterous. In this case we are fit only to be excluded. Yet in spite of what we are, God loves us. Indeed, he has proved his own unique love for us in that, while we were sinful, ungodly, helpless and even the enemies of God, Christ died for us (Rom 5:6-10). It is all but unbelievable. Yet it is true. To deny it is to constitute ourselves "enemies of the cross of Christ" (Phil 3:18); to confess it is to join the company of those who will spend eternity worshiping "the Lamb, who was slain" (Rev 5:12).

Justification by Faith

The cross was a multifaceted achievement and has many different meanings. It is the ultimate revelation of God's love and justice. It is the decisive conquest of evil. It is the ground of our salvation. It is the supreme example of self-sacrifice. It is the most powerful inspiration to Christian devotion. Moreover, the salvation won by the cross is illustrated in the New Testament by a variety of metaphors like propitiation, redemption and reconciliation. But evangelical Christians have always insisted that the richest model is justification.

"Justification by faith" was the watchword of the Protestant Reformation. Luther called it "the principal article of all Christian doctrine, which maketh true Christians indeed."[18] And Thomas Cranmer wrote in his eloquent homily "Of the Salvation of Mankind":

This faith the holy Scripture teacheth: this is the strong rock and foundation of Christian religion: this doctrine all old and ancient authors of

Christ's church do approve: this doctrine advanceth and setteth forth the true glory of Christ, and beateth down the vain glory of man: this whosoever denieth is not to be counted for a true Christian man, nor for a setter forth of Christ's glory, but for an adversary of Christ and his gospel, and for a setter forth of men's vainglory.[19]

To these sixteenth-century statements I add a statement of some contemporary Anglican evangelicals:

Justification by Faith appears to us, as it does to all evangelicals, to be the heart and hub, the paradigm and essence, of the whole economy of God's saving grace. Like Atlas, it bears a world on its shoulders, the entire evangelical knowledge of God's love in Christ towards sinners.[20]

So what is justification? It is of course a legal word, borrowed from the law courts, and the opposite of condemnation. When God justifies sinners, he declares a verdict, in anticipation of the last day, that he has not only forgiven all their sins but granted them a righteous standing of acceptance in his sight.

There are five aspects of justification in the New Testament which we need to keep clear in our minds.

First, *its source*. We are "justified freely by his grace" (Rom 3:24). God's grace is his free and spontaneous love, undeserved, undesired and unsolicited. So what grace gives it gives *gratis*, "for nothing," as Augustine often repeated. Grace-gifts are *gratis*-gifts.

Second, *its ground*. We have been "justified by his blood" (Rom 5:9), that is, on account of his sacrificial death. The reason why "there is now no condemnation for those who are in Christ Jesus" (Rom 8:1) is that God "condemned sin" in Jesus (Rom 8:3). We are justified because *he* was condemned. The law has no claims on us because they were all met at the cross.

Third, *its sphere*. We are "justified in Christ" (Gal 2:17). This is a neglected phrase. It means that we are justified only when we are united to Christ, and of course when we are united to Christ we are part of his new community and committed to living a new life.

Fourth, *its means*. We are "justified by faith." This is the most frequently repeated of the expressions about justification in Paul's letters (see, e.g., Rom 3:28; 5:1; Gal 2:16; Phil 3:9). It was a sure instinct of Luther's to add the word *alone* to his translation of the Greek of Romans 3:28, as several early church fathers had done before him. Since our justification is altogether "apart from observing the law," it must be by faith alone. In saying so, however, we must be careful not to turn our faith into another work. We are indeed justified by God's grace and by Christ's blood, but only *through* faith. To say "justification by faith alone" is another way of saying "justification by Christ alone." Faith has no function but to receive what grace freely offers. As the judicious Richard Hooker put it with his usual precision, "God doth justify the believing man, yet not for the worthiness of his belief, but for his worthiness who is believed."[21] Faith is nothing but the hand which takes the gift, the eye which beholds the giver, and the mouth which drinks the water of life.

Fifth, *its fruit*. We are saved unto good works. "For it is by grace you have been saved, through faith . . . not by works, so that no one can boast. For we are God's workmanship, created in Christ Jesus to do good works" (Eph 2:8-10). These verses make abundantly plain the place of good works in justification. Justification is not *by* works but *unto* good works. Put differently, salvation is through faith, but faith works through love (Gal 5:6).

Here then is the grand doctrine of justification. Its origin is God's grace and its ground Christ's blood. The sphere of its enjoyment is Christ, its means is faith, and its fruit good works. It was of such central importance to Paul that he was prepared even to suffer the acute embarrassment of a public showdown with his brother apostle Peter rather than compromise what he called "the truth of the gospel," which we might call "the evangelical faith" (Gal 2:11-17).

If justification by faith was one of the watchwords of the Reformation, it was also one of its chief points of debate with Rome. Roman Catholics were (and still are) disturbed by the Reformers' teaching. In particular, they disagreed with the Reformers' insistence that justification denoted a legal pronouncement and not a moral change. This seemed to them a legal fiction which left the sinner unchanged and which therefore was antinomian in tendency. So the Council of Trent, summarizing the Counter-Reformation, taught that justification includes both forgiveness and renewal, and that the baptized person is cleansed from all sins (both original and actual) and is simultaneously infused with a new and supernatural righteousness.

The controversy continues. Evangelicals maintain that their doctrine is not antinomian but the opposite. It generates righteousness. While still insisting that "to justify" means "to declare" and not "to make" righteous, evangelicals emphasize that justification is always accompanied by regeneration. Everybody whom God justifies he simultaneously regenerates. Moreover, this new birth leads inevitably to a new life, this justification to sanctification.

It would certainly make for clarity if we remembered five fundamental differences between justification and sanctification, which the Puritans used to emphasize.

1. Justification is God's judicial verdict, declaring a sinner righteous; sanctification is his moral activity, making a sinner righteous.

2. God justifies sinners through the death of his Son, but sanctifies them through the regeneration and indwelling of his Holy Spirit.

3. Justification is instantaneous. It takes place immediately when God pronounces the sinner righteous. Sanctification, however, is gradual. It begins the moment we are justified, but then it grows as the Holy Spirit transforms us into the image of Christ (2 Cor 3:18).

4. Justification is complete. It has no degrees. We shall not be more justified on the day of our death than we were on the day of our conversion. Sanctification, however, is incomplete. Although it begins when we are converted and regenerated, it continues throughout our life on

earth and will be complete when Christ appears. Only then "we shall be like him, for we shall see him as he is" (1 Jn 3:2).

5. Justification is by faith only without works. It is entirely the work of Christ. But sanctification is by faith and works. In addition to trusting God, we are told to watch and pray, to sanctify and purify ourselves.

To sum up, God declares us righteous through the death of his Son, by faith only, so that our justification is both instantaneous and complete. But God makes us righteous through the indwelling of his Spirit, by faith and works, so that our sanctification is both gradual and incomplete.

OUR DAILY DISCIPLESHIP

We now return to our text (Gal 6:14 REB), "God forbid that I should boast of anything but the cross of our Lord Jesus Christ, through which the world is crucified to me and I to the world!" It is evident that we glory in the cross not only for our acceptance with God but for our daily discipleship. The cross is the way of holiness as well as the way of forgiveness.

Notice that, although Paul mentions only one cross, he refers to three crucifixions on it. First, there is of course the crucifixion of Jesus. Second, "the world has been crucified to me." Third, "I [have been crucified] to the world." Thus Jesus Christ, the godless world and we ourselves have all been crucified on the same cross. Paul has already introduced us to this notion in earlier verses of his letter. In Galatians 2:20 he has written, "I have been crucified with Christ and I no longer live, but Christ lives in me." Then in Galatians 5:24 he has written, "Those who belong to Christ Jesus have crucified [their] sinful nature with its passions and desires." Although there are different nuances between these statements, they express the same fundamental truth. I would express it like this: Christ died as our *substitute*, instead of us, so that we might not have to die for our sins (as the New Testament obliges us to affirm), but he also died as our *representative*, so that when he died we died with him.

This is Paul's elaboration of the call of Jesus to take up our cross and follow him (e.g., Mk 8:34). If we had lived in those days in Palestine, when the country was occupied by Roman soldiers, and if we had seen a man walking down the road carrying a cross, or at least the *patibulum* or cross-bar, we would not have needed to run up to him, tap him on the shoulder, and say, "Excuse me, sir, but what on earth are you doing?" We would have recognized him at once as a condemned criminal on his way to execution. The Romans compelled any man they condemned to the cross to carry it to the scene of crucifixion.

Now Christ calls us to deny ourselves, take up our cross, and follow him. If then we are carrying a cross and following Christ, there is only one place to which we can be going, namely to death. Dietrich Bonhoeffer, the Lutheran pastor who died in a Nazi concentration camp in April 1945, wrote in his justly famous book *The Cost of Discipleship*, "When Christ calls a man, he bids him come and die."[22] Thus cross-bearing and crucifixion were Jesus' dramatic images of self-denial. They come into direct collision with the human potential movement, to which I have already referred, with its teaching about self-actualization and self-esteem, and indeed with every form of self-centeredness.

To be sure, Jesus did teach that his followers would find themselves and fulfill themselves. But he added that the only road to self-discovery is self-denial, the only way to find ourselves is to lose ourselves, and the only way to live is to die to our own self-centeredness. This teaching is extremely important today, because the church has a constant tendency to trivialize Christian discipleship. People think of it as if it means nothing more than becoming a bit religious, and adding a thin layer of piety to an otherwise secular life. Then scratch the surface or prick the veneer, and underneath there is the same old pagan. Nothing fundamental has changed.

But no! Becoming and being a Christian involves a change so radical that no imagery can do it justice but death and resurrection with Christ, namely dying to the old life of self-indulgence and self-will, and rising to a new life of self-control and self-giving, in which the world has been crucified to us and we have been crucified to the world. We glory in the cross for our discipleship.

OUR MISSION AND MESSAGE

The Christian church is called to mission, but there can be no mission without a message. So what is our message for the world? It centers on the cross, on the fantastic truth of a God who loves us, and who gave himself for us in Christ on the cross.

Consider what Paul has written earlier. He has described his earlier ministry in Galatia in these terms: "Before your very eyes Jesus Christ was clearly portrayed as crucified" (Gal 3:1). That is, the cross had been the focus of his message. He had placarded Christ crucified before their eyes as if on a public billboard. The Galatians had not of course seen Christ die. They lived about a thousand miles by land from Jerusalem. So far as we know, Paul had not seen him die either. But through the preaching of the cross the apostle had brought the past into the present and made the historical event of the cross a contemporary reality to them. This is also what the Lord's Supper or the Eucharist does. The technical word for it is *anamnēsis*, or remembrance, as word and sacrament together dramatize verbally and visually the unique, epoch-making event of the cross.

In consequence of his striking presentation, Paul had enabled the Galatians to see the cross in their imagination, to understand that he had died for their sins, to kneel before the cross in great humility, and to receive from the hands of the crucified Savior the gift of eternal life, which was absolutely free and utterly undeserved. But this preaching of the cross, as Paul was later to elaborate in 1 Corinthians, is a stumbling block to human pride. It undermines our self-righteousness. It insists that we cannot achieve our salvation by anything that we do. Indeed, we cannot even contribute to it. How we would love to be able to do so! How we would enjoy strutting round heaven like peacocks, displaying our gorgeous plumage! If only we could claim salvation as a well-deserved prize! But no, salvation is a totally noncontributory gift. As William Temple put it, "All is of God; the only thing of my very own which I can contribute to my own redemption is the sin from which I need to be redeemed."[23] We find the cross humiliating, as it strips us naked and declares us bankrupt before God. It is in this connection that Paul contrasts himself with those false teachers we call the Judaizers. They "preached circumcision" (which is apostolic shorthand for self-salvation by obedience to the law), and so they escaped persecution for the cross of Christ. He, on the other hand, preached Christ crucified (that is, salvation through the cross alone), and so was always being persecuted (Gal 5:11; 6:12).

The same choice confronts all Christian communicators today. On the one hand, we can flatter people and tell them what they want to hear, namely that they are fine people and can win salvation by their own effort. We develop what could be called a pussy-cat ministry, for we stroke them until they purr with pleasure. Or, on the other hand, we can tell them the truth which they don't want to hear, about sin, guilt, judgment and the cross, and so arouse their hostility. In other words, either we are unfaithful in order to be popular, or we are willing to be unpopular in our determination to be faithful. I doubt very much if it is possible to be faithful and popular at the same time. I fear that we have to choose.

It is extraordinary how much hostility there is to the gospel of the cross. One example is the late Alfred Ayer, Oxford philosopher, exponent of logical positivism, author of *Language, Truth and Logic*, and outspoken critic of the Christian faith. He wrote in 1979 that there was quite a strong case for considering Christianity the worst of the religions of historical importance. Why? Because it rests "on the allied doctrines of original sin and vicarious atonement, which are intellectually contemptible and morally outrageous."[24]

My thesis has been that for our acceptance with God, for our daily discipleship, and for our mission and message to the world, we like Paul

should glory in nothing but the cross. We human beings are born boast-
ers. There seems to be something in our inherited constitution which in-
clines us to boasting. We seem to need to glory in something, in order to
inflate our ego. In consequence, we boast of our education, our posses-
sions, our success, our reputation, even our piety. We find it hard to learn
C. H. Spurgeon's dictum "Be not proud of race, face, place or grace."

But in the last resort there is only one alternative before us. Either we
glory in ourselves and in our own achievements, or we glory in Christ
and in his achievement on the cross. There is no possibility of compromise. A hallmark of authentic evangelical Christianity is that we glory
only in the cross.

SUGGESTED FURTHER READING

Boice, James, and Philip G. Ryken. *The Heart of the Cross.* Wheaton, Ill.:
    Crossway, 1999.

Bruce, F. F. *Jesus: Lord and Savior.* Downers Grove, Ill.: InterVarsity Press,
    1986.

Morris, Leon. *The Atonement.* Downers Grove, Ill.: InterVarsity Press,
    1983.

Sproul, R. C. *Mighty Christ.* Darlington, U.K.: Evangelical Press, 1995.

Stott, John. *The Cross of Christ.* Downers Grove, Ill.: InterVarsity Press,
    1986.

3

The Ministry of the Holy Spirit

WE LOOKED IN THE INTRODUCTION AT DIFFERENT ATTEMPTS to summarize the leading features of evangelicalism. Each began with the supremacy of Scripture and the majesty of Christ, particularly of his cross. Some continued with the lordship of the Holy Spirit. Others added one or more of the following five distinctives: the necessity of conversion, the priority of evangelism, the importance of fellowship, the longing for revival and the search for holiness.

My own concern is to establish a firm trinitarian base for the evangelical faith, and then to add the other five concerns relating to conversion, evangelism, fellowship, revival and holiness not as extras but as aspects of the ministry of the Holy Spirit, for they are all certainly his concerns. Thus the Bible, the cross and the Spirit become the fundamental triad of evangelical essentials. Or, put differently, in such a way as to honor the three persons of the Trinity, the evangelical faith focuses on the revelation of God, the cross of Christ and the ministry of the Spirit. Further, alluding to a distinction made in the introduction, the Bible and the cross belong to the category of the *hapax* ("once for all"), while the Spirit also belongs to the *mallon* ("more and more"). It is he who enables us to enter ever more fully into what God has said and done in Christ.

The Holy Spirit has sometimes been referred to as the "neglected" member of the Trinity. But, at least among evangelical and Reformed people, this is not an altogether accurate judgment. Evangelicals have always sought to honor the Spirit. Calvin has been called the theologian of the Spirit, and two of the finest and fullest treatises ever written on the work of the Spirit were *Pneumatologia: A Discourse Concerning the Holy Spirit* (1674) by the great Puritan leader John Owen and *The Work of the Holy Spirit* (1900) by Dutch Reformed theologian and statesman Abraham Kuyper.

The twentieth century, however, witnessed an unfortunate disagreement among evangelical Christians about the work of the Holy Spirit, with the rise of modern Pentecostal churches at the beginning of the century, and of the charismatic movement in the mainline churches since the 1950s. Evangelical leaders have been divided over these phenomena, and in consequence it has become a very sensitive subject. On the one hand, there is the recognition that Pentecostalism is today the fastest-growing Christian movement in the world, providing abundant evidence of God's blessing upon it. On the other hand, there is genuine anxiety that it is often growth without depth, so that there is much superficiality everywhere. My personal conviction is that what unites evangelicals in our doctrine and experience of the Holy Spirit is considerably greater than what divides us, and my concern in this chapter is to concentrate on the former while not concealing the latter.

I see that in the previous paragraph I have used the two adjectives *evangelical* and *charismatic* without defining them in relation to each other. The purpose of this book is of course to define the word *evangelical,* but what does *charismatic* mean? In a general sense all Christians are charismatics, inasmuch as the church is the charismatic body of Christ, each member of his body having been endowed with a spiritual gift (*charisma*) or gifts (*charismata*). In particular, however, the term *charismatic* is applied to those members of mainline denominations (a) who claim a "charismatic" experience, subsequent to conversion, which is usually called "the baptism of the Spirit," (b) who lay special emphasis on three supernatural gifts, namely tongues, healing and prophecy, and (c) who develop a style of public worship which is exuberant, spontaneous, participatory and demonstrative.

It will be seen, therefore, that not all evangelicals are charismatic (since some emphasize the new birth rather than subsequent experiences, and point out that the gifts mentioned in the New Testament number more than twenty, not all of which are supernatural), while not all charismatics are evangelical (since some are Anglican Catholics or Roman Catholics). It is important to remember in the rest of this chapter that *evangelical* and *charismatic* are not synonyms.

We begin with the statement that all evangelical Christians firmly believe in the Holy Spirit, the gracious and glorious third person of the Trinity. We believe that he is God, and therefore worthy of worship. We also believe both that he was active in creating all things (Gen 1:2) and that he is active in sustaining, animating and renewing all things (Ps 104:30). We believe that in Old Testament days he was both regenerating the people of God, for otherwise they could not have loved God's law (cf. Ps 119:97, 103; Rom 7:22; 8:7), and equipping special people for special tasks (e.g., Ex 35:30ff. and 2 Pet 1:21). As for New Testament days, in which we are privileged to live, we strongly affirm that the ministry of the Holy Spirit is literally indispensable, since no aspect of our Christian faith, life, worship, fellowship, service or mission would be possible without him, as this chapter will seek to demonstrate.

Another introductory emphasis which needs to be made is that we should avoid any tendency—voluntary or involuntary—to separate the Holy Spirit from the Father or the Son. We declare again that the evangelical faith is the trinitarian faith, and the more we learn to think and act as trinitarian Christians, the more authentically evangelical we shall be. Although it is impossible for our finite minds to understand the precise relations between the three persons of the Trinity, it is essential to remember that they enjoy both equality within the Godhead and distinct roles. For example, the Holy Spirit loves to efface himself in order to honor the Father and the Son—which is not surprising since he is called both "the Spirit of God" and "the Spirit of Christ" (e.g., Rom 8:9; Gal 4:6). Thus, it is he who, when we pray, enables us to cry, "*Abba*, Father," and so to appreciate our filial relationship to him (Rom 8:15-16). It is also he who enables us to cry, "Jesus is Lord." Indeed, "no one can say, 'Jesus is Lord,' except by the Holy Spirit" (1 Cor 12:3).

That the Spirit delights to witness to the Son is much stressed in the New Testament, not least by Jesus himself. He said, "He [the Spirit of truth] will glorify me, for he will take what is mine and make it known to you. All that the Father has is mine, and that is why I said, 'He will take what is mine and make it known to you'" (Jn 16:14-15 REB). So then, a reliable test of the genuineness of every person and movement claiming the endorsement of the Holy Spirit is whether they honor the Lord Jesus Christ, draw attention to him and promote his glory. Several recent authors have illustrated this by calling the ministry of the Holy Spirit a "floodlight" ministry. The essence of good floodlighting is to illuminate a building while keeping the lamps concealed. Just so, the Holy Spirit witnesses to Christ while himself remaining hidden.

Perhaps the best way to grasp the indispensability of the work of the Spirit is to consider in turn the six main stages or aspects of Christian discipleship, beginning with the new birth and ending with the Christian hope, and to show how each would be impossible apart from the operation of the Holy Spirit.

CHRISTIAN BEGINNINGS

Some Christian historians and commentators, as we have seen, regard "conversion" or "conversionism" as one of evangelicalism's main distinctives. Some even talk about "an evangelical conversion experience," as if there were a stereotype—probably like that of Saul on the Damascus road—to which everybody is expected to conform. We must emphatically reject this. Although every true conversion includes a personal encounter with Jesus Christ, several aspects of Saul's conversion (e.g., the blinding light, the fall to the ground and the voice speaking Aramaic) were atypical. My decided preference, when thinking about Christian beginnings, is to refer to *regeneration* rather than *conversion* as an evangelical essential. Although the two may coincide, they are fundamentally different in that conversion is a human work (although possible only by the enabling grace of God), whereas regeneration is entirely a work of God. Conversion denotes that turn from sin and idolatry which we call repentance, together with that turn to God and to Christ which we call faith. The resulting equation is that repentance plus faith equals conversion. Regeneration or new birth, however, is different.

Unfortunately the subject has recently been trivialized, especially in the United States, so that statistics are now published of those claiming to be "born-again Christians." Yet the birth metaphor gives us several important clues, leading to a correct understanding.

First, *the new birth is a work of God.* As with physical birth, so with spiritual birth, nobody has ever given birth to himself. Regeneration is not self-generated. So the new birth is not merely a moral reformation, although it leads to one. In his nighttime conversation with Nicodemus, Jesus twice spoke of being born *anōthen*, an adverb which could mean either "from the beginning, again" or "from above" (Jn 3:3, 7). The latter is regarded as more probable in this context. In this case Jesus was referring not to a new beginning from below by human effort but to a new birth from above by the power of God. In fact, the new birth is birth of the Spirit (Jn 3:5-8).

Second, *the new birth is sudden.* Although human birth is preceded by nine months of gestation and is followed by years of development into maturity, birth itself is a more or less instantaneous event. So with the new birth. Months may precede it, in which the Holy Spirit is convicting of sin (Jn 16:8-11), pricking the conscience (see Acts 26:14) and illumining the mind. And years of Christian growth will follow. But the actual new birth (or passage from death to life) is instantaneous.

Third, *the new birth is not necessarily a conscious experience*, although it is for some. Conversion, the turning process, is likely to be conscious, but not the moment when God puts life within us. Again the birth metaphor demonstrates this. We were not conscious of our own birth experience. We would not know our birthday unless our parents had told us; we were not aware at the time what was happening. Similarly, many Christians do not know their spiritual birthday.

Fourth, *the new birth is not identical with baptism*. To identify them is a mistake often made by Catholics (both Anglican and Roman) who imagine that, because they have been baptized, they must have been born again. Of course, baptism is very important. Jesus himself instituted and commanded it (Mt 28:19), so evangelicals do not (or should not) minimize it. But we strongly insist that baptism must never be confused with the new birth. Indeed, if Jesus' conversation with Nicodemus was historical (as we believe it was), then his reference to being "born of water and the Spirit" (Jn 3:5) cannot possibly have been an allusion to Christian baptism, since at that time it did not exist. It is more likely to have alluded to John's baptism and call to repentance, since at that very time John the Baptist was himself making the distinction between water and Spirit (Mt 3:11), between his baptism with water and Jesus' baptism with the Spirit.

So then, although baptism is a sign (or "sacrament") of the new birth, we must not confuse the sign with the thing signified. The new birth is a deep, inward, radical change worked by the Holy Spirit in the inner recesses of the human personality, by which we receive a new life, a new heart, a new beginning. Baptism, however, is a visible and public dramatization of this inward and secret reality of the new birth.

Further, baptism does not automatically effect what it signifies. Evangelical Christians reject a mechanical view of either of the two gospel sacraments, baptism and the Lord's Supper. The administration of water in baptism does not convey the new birth, nor do the bread and wine of Communion convey the body and blood of Christ. True, the Council of

Trent pronounced an anathema on anybody who "shall affirm that grace is not conferred by these sacraments . . . by their own power [*ex opere operato*]."[1] But this is exactly what we do affirm. As Richard Hooker put it later, "All receive not the grace of God who receive the sacraments of his grace."[2] If the sacraments are to benefit us, they must be received "rightly" (see *Anglican Articles* 26-27), and "rightly" means "by faith." It is important for members of free and new churches to understand that, for Anglican evangelicals, baptism (whether of infants or of adults) lacks efficacy if it is not accompanied by faith. I do not know anybody who has put this more forcefully than James Ussher, who became archbishop of Armagh in 1625:

> As baptism administered to those of years is not effectual unless they believe, so we can make no comfortable use of our baptism administered in our infancy until we believe. . . . All the promises of grace were in my baptism estated upon me, and sealed up unto me, on God's part; but then I come to have the profit and benefit of them when I come to understand what grant God, in baptism, hath sealed unto me, and actually to lay hold on it by faith.[3]

Finally, before we leave the topic of Christian beginnings, we note that the lesson most emphatically taught by Jesus in his conversation with Nicodemus was the indispensable necessity of the new birth. Nicodemus was a Jew (belonging to God's covenant people), a Pharisee (committed to righteousness), a leader (a member of the Sanhedrin), a teacher (a person of culture), and polite and appreciative in his evaluation of the ministry of Jesus. He was religious, moral, educated and courteous. Yet it was to him that Jesus said, "You should not be surprised at my saying, 'You must be born again'" (Jn 3:7). Evangelical Christians have always tried to be loyal to this teaching of Jesus, and to insist both that the new birth is indispensable if we are ever to see or enter God's kingdom and that baptism is no substitute for it.

CHRISTIAN ASSURANCE

The Holy Spirit does not bring about the new birth and then abandon us. He knows, as all parents know, that newborn babies need careful nurture. So he stays with us. Better still, he dwells in us. In consequence, birth of the Spirit is followed by life in the Spirit. We now consider some of the blessings of this new life, and in particular the blessing of Christian assurance.

During his last evening on earth, surrounded by his apostles, Jesus said:

> Nevertheless I tell you the truth: it is to your advantage that I go away, for if I do not go away, the Advocate [NIV "Counselor"] will not come to you; but if I go, I will send him to you. (Jn 16:7 NRSV)

Here is Jesus' plain statement that the ministry of the Holy Spirit would be more advantageous to the apostles than his own earthly ministry had been. Many people are utterly astonished by these words. How could it possibly be to the apostles' advantage, or in their best interests, that he should go away and leave them behind? We look on the apostles with envy. If only we could have been with Jesus, as they were! If only we could have seen the beauty of his face and heard the music of his voice! If only we could have watched him feed the hungry, heal the sick, still the storm, and raise the dead! If only we could have sat at his feet like Mary of Bethany or leaned on his breast like John the beloved disciple! What can Jesus have meant?

Well, the apostles experienced two major disadvantages during Jesus' earthly life, which would be overcome by the arrival of the Spirit. First, while Jesus was with them on earth, his presence was localized. In consequence, they were sometimes separated from him, for example when he was in Jerusalem and they were in Galilee, or when he was praying on the mountain and they were in the boat. They could not enjoy uninterrupted fellowship with Jesus. His presence was limited to one place at a time. But what the Holy Spirit has done is to *universalize* the presence of Jesus, to make him available to everybody everywhere.

The apostles' second disadvantage, while Jesus was with them on earth, was that his presence was external to them. He was not able to enter their personality and change them from within. He could not get at the source of their thoughts, motives and desires, but later he would, he said, for "he lives with you, and will be in you" (Jn 14:17). Thus the Holy Spirit *internalizes* the presence of Jesus, so that now he dwells by his Spirit in our hearts (Eph 3:16-17) and our body is the temple of the Holy Spirit (1 Cor 6:19).

This indwelling of the Holy Spirit is the most marvelous privilege. It has always been emphasized by evangelical Christians, and it is also the chief difference between his Old Testament and his New Testament ministries. Although the Old Testament people of God were regenerate, it does not seem that the Spirit indwelt them. At least they looked forward to the messianic age as the time when God would fulfil his promise, "I will put my Spirit in you" (Ezek 36:27). It is this promise which Jesus confirmed.

I think all evangelical Christians agree and affirm that the indwelling presence of the Holy Spirit is the chief distinguishing mark of the people of God today, so that "if anyone does not have the Spirit of Christ, he does not belong to Christ" (Rom 8:9). Paul also urges us not to grieve the Holy Spirit, with whom we have been "sealed" for the day of redemption (Eph 4:30). Thus, the Holy Spirit within us is God's seal, branding us as belonging to him. This emphasis on the inwardness of the Spirit's work enables us to say that evangelical religion is heart religion. "The fourth leading feature in Evangelical Religion," wrote Bishop J. C. Ryle (after the supremacy of Scripture, the depth of human sinfulness and the salvation of Jesus Christ), "is the high place which it assigns to the inward work of the Holy Spirit in the heart of man."[4]

There is of course a place for externals in religion. But throughout history there has been a constant tendency for religion to degenerate into an empty show. God complained through Isaiah, "These people come near to me with their mouth, and honor me with their lips, but their hearts are far from me" (Is 29:13). And what Yahweh said to eighth-century Israel, Jesus reapplied to the Pharisees of his own day (Mk 7:6), and we need to reapply to ourselves today. Too much of our religion is ritual without reality, the mouth without the heart, "having a form of godliness but denying its power" (2 Tim 3:5).

One of the main ministries of the indwelling Spirit is to give God's people an assurance of their saving relationship to him. The doctrine of assurance is, in fact, a specifically evangelical emphasis.[5] Those of Catholic or liberal persuasion tend to regard what we call *assurance* as a synonym for a horrid form of presumption. And, to be honest, we evangelical people do need to repent of our rather cocky, self-assured and even triumphalist attitudes. We need to heed the warnings of John's first letter, to the effect that all our claims to know God and to be his children are bogus unless we are characterized by righteousness and love in addition to Christological orthodoxy.

Yet the constant repetition in John's first letter of statements like "we know that we have come to know him," "we know we are in him," "we know that we have passed from death to life" and "we know that we are children of God" (see 1 Jn 2:3, 5; 3:14, 19; 4:13; 5:19) leaves us in no doubt that God intends us to know, in other words to have assurance, that we belong to him.

Christian assurance rests first and foremost on the cross. It is because Christ bore our sins in our place, and because his sin-bearing was finished and complete, that we may know we have been forgiven. Christ made on the cross "by his one oblation of himself once offered" what the 1662 *Prayer Book* calls "a full, perfect, and sufficient sacrifice, oblation, and satisfaction, for the sins of the whole world."[6] To this objective ground of our assurance the Holy Spirit adds his own subjective testimony. The clearest statements of it are given in Romans. In Romans 5:5 we are told that through the Holy Spirit given to us, God has poured out his love in our hearts. In Romans 8:15-16 we are told that when we cry, "*Abba*, Father," it is the Spirit himself who is witnessing with our spirit that we are God's children. Thus the indwelling Spirit assures us deeply in our hearts that God is our Father and that he loves us. Moreover, the context makes it plain that this inward experience of the outpoured love of our Father is a privilege which should be common to all his children, although surely different Christians receive this assurance in different degrees at different times.

Since many have linked these experiences with the so-called baptism of the Spirit, this may be an appropriate place in which to broach the subject. It is a divisive issue. Pentecostal and charismatic Christians tend to insist that the baptism of the Spirit is a necessary second experience, subsequent to the new birth, and that it is normally validated by speaking in tongues. Non-Pentecostal people believe rather that the baptism of the Spirit is identical with the gift of the Spirit (Acts 1:5; 2:33, 38-39), and that it is given to all believers, although subsequent experiences of different kinds are often given.

Is it really necessary for evangelical Christians to be divided on this issue by an excess of rigidity? Pentecostal Christians need to ask themselves whether they must insist on a two-stage stereotype. Non-Pentecostal Christians, who claim to have received the Spirit once for all at their conversion, need to ask themselves whether they are sufficiently open to further and fuller experiences of him. Would it not be possible for both sides to agree (1) that all Christians have received the Holy Spirit; (2) that the New Testament emphasis is on this initial reception of the Spirit, associated with the vocabulary of new birth, new creation and resurrection from the dead; (3) that the process of sanctification follows this; and (4) that during this process many richer, deeper, fuller experiences of the Spirit may be granted?

I venture to close this section with a personal anecdote. I have several times been the privileged guest of the Anglican diocese of Singapore. During a visit there in 1987 I was speaking with my host, Bishop (later Archbishop) Moses Tay, a well-known charismatic evangelical. I asked him what in his view the essence of renewal was. He replied, "It's a new experience of the presence of God." I was immediately struck by this, because I had recently read J. I. Packer's book *Keep in Step with the Spirit* (1984) and had come across his expression "a fresh assurance of the love of God." There seems to me very little difference between "a new experience of the presence of God" and "a fresh assurance of the love of God." I found myself wondering if this could be the basis for greater mutual understanding and respect.

CHRISTIAN HOLINESS

One of the major purposes of the Holy Spirit's indwelling of his people is to change or sanctify them. God's Old Testament promise "I will put my Spirit in you" continues: "and move you to follow my decrees and be careful to keep my laws" (Ezek 36:27). In fact, God's two most direct Old Testament promises were these:

- I will put my Spirit in you. (Ezek 36:27)
- I will put my law in their minds. (Jer 31:33)

There is no fundamental difference between these promises, since what the Spirit does when he is put within us is to write God's law there (cf. Rom 8:3-4). Paul emphasized the same indissoluble link between the Holy Spirit and the holy people he indwells when he wrote that the God who calls us "to live a holy life" also "gives [us] his Holy Spirit" (1 Thess 4:7-8). With the Holy Spirit holiness is essential; without the Holy Spirit holiness is impossible. So we must not underestimate what he can do in effecting real change, giving us new ambitions, new standards, new ideals and new values.

But how does such change come about? It is here that Paul introduces us, in both Galatians 5 and Romans 8, to the unrelenting inner conflict which we experience between "the flesh" and "the Spirit." By "the flesh" he means our fallen, self-indulgent nature, and by "the Spirit" the indwelling Holy Spirit himself. The secret of holiness, he tells us, lies in our adopting right attitudes to both. Our negative attitude to "the flesh" is properly called *mortification,* the process of putting it to death. It is a much neglected practice among us. "I am more and more convinced," wrote Martyn Lloyd-Jones, "that most people get into trouble in the living of the Christian life because of their molly-coddling of themselves spiritually."[7] That is, we pamper our selfish nature instead of executing it.

Here is Paul's most outspoken statement of the alternative before us:

> For if you live according to the sinful nature, you will die; but if by the Spirit you put to death the misdeeds of the body, you will live. (Rom 8:13)

Here are set over against each other a kind of life which issues in death and a kind of death which issues in life. First, the alternative lifestyles are "living according to the sinful nature" (which is indulgence) and "putting to death the misdeeds of the body" (which is mortification). Second, the alternative consequences are death and life: if we indulge ourselves we will die, but if we mortify ourselves we will live. And third, there are alternative combatants: on our own we indulge ourselves, but through the Spirit we mortify ourselves. In other words, we are called to a radical, uncompromising rejection of everything we know to be evil in God's sight. It is our responsibility; we are to do it. But we cannot do it by ourselves, only through the power of the indwelling Spirit.

But what does this mean? It is pious, orthodox language, no doubt. But how in everyday experience does the Holy Spirit work within us? I have found it helpful, in my own thinking and struggling, to spell out a "5-D" formula, that is, five steps or stages in the sanctifying activity of the Holy Spirit. He operates (1) in our mind, enabling us to *discern* the will of God; (2) in our conscience, enabling us to *distinguish* between right and wrong; (3) in our heart, enabling us to *desire* God's way ardently; and (4) in our will, enabling us to *determine* resolutely to follow God's will. The fifth "D" (*do*) can only then take place.

The apostle also writes of holiness as "the fruit of the Spirit," nine graces which together constitute Christlikeness of character and conduct. As "fruit" they ripen naturally, under the indwelling influence of the Spirit. Christian holiness is not a Christmas-tree phenomenon, whose decorations are tied on artificially; it is fruit-tree holiness, that is, natural development, provided that we "walk in the Spirit" (Gal 5:16 KJV), responding to his promptings and living under his control.

There has been a long-standing emphasis on holiness in the Catholic tradition, so that evangelicals cannot in any way claim a monopoly of it. We can say, however, that the history of evangelicalism has been a history of the search for sanctification. We find it in every century—in the Reformers, the Puritans, the Pietists, the Methodists and, more recently, in such movements as that associated with the Keswick Convention. No one type of holiness teaching has predominated among evangelical Christians. Sometimes a perfectionist movement has developed, promising the "eradication" of our fallen nature or "entire sanctification" or "perfect love." And one can only admire the resolve to take seriously those New Testament passages which either command perfection (e.g., Mt 5:48; 2 Cor 7:1) or state that those born of God "do not," even "cannot" sin (1 Jn 3:6, 9; 5:18).

John Wesley wrestled long with such texts and wrote his conclusions in *A Plain Account of Christian Perfection* (definitive edition, 1777). The tradition continues today in the Free Methodist, Nazarene and Pentecostal churches. But most evangelicals, interpreting "perfectionist" texts in their context, are convinced that neither the eradication of evil nor the possibility of sinless perfection is promised in the New Testament for this life. Rather, we are on a journey, pilgrims heading for the celestial city. Like Paul we have not yet arrived, nor "been made perfect," but we are pressing on "to take hold of that for which Christ Jesus took hold of [us]" (Phil 3:12).

Handley Moule, who was the first principal of Ridley Hall in Cambridge and who later became the evangelical bishop of Durham, succeeded in maintaining a biblical balance in his little book *Thoughts on Christian Sanctity* (1888). Under the heading "Aims" he wrote:

We aim at nothing less than to walk with God all day long; to abide every hour in Christ; to love God with all the heart and our neighbour as ourselves . . . to "yield our selves to God" . . . to break with all evil, and follow all good. . . . We are absolutely bound to put quite aside all secret purposes of moral compromise; all tolerance of besetting sin. . . . We cannot possibly rest short of a daily, hourly, continuous walk with God, in Christ, by the grace of the Holy Ghost.[8]

Under "Limits," however, Bishop Moule went on to write:

I hold with absolute conviction, alike from the experience of the church and from the infallible Word, that, in the mystery of things, there will be limits to the last, and very humbling limits, very real fallings short. To the last it will be a sinner that walks with God.[9]

With these "aims" and "limits" in mind, and seeking the continuous fullness of the Spirit (Eph 5:18), evangelical Christians "hunger and thirst for righteousness" (Mt 5:6).

CHRISTIAN COMMUNITY

Evangelical Christians have the reputation of being rugged individualists, and so of having an inadequate doctrine of the church. It is certainly true that, since the Reformation, we have insisted both on "the right of private judgment" (the privilege of making up our own mind from Scripture) and on "the priesthood of all believers" (the privilege of an immediate, individual access to God through Christ). But we also know that the New Testament has a very high doctrine of the church; that the church is at the center of the eternal and historical purpose of God; and that the church is part of the gospel. The church also enjoys a direct continuity with Old Testament Israel. It is not therefore strictly correct to refer to the Day of Pentecost as "the birthday of the church." For the church as the covenant people of God came into being some two thousand years previously with Abraham. What happened at Pentecost was that the people of God became the Spirit-filled body of Christ. It is also called "the fellowship of the Holy Spirit" (2 Cor 13:14; cf. Phil 2:1) because it is our common participation (*koinōnia*) in him which constitutes us the church.

The term *koinōnia* does not occur in the Gospels. Its first appearance is in Acts 2:42, Luke's description of the Jerusalem church, because there could be no *koinōnia* before the Spirit came. There has always been a degree of disagreement and tension within the evangelical movement about the nature of the church. Some affirm that it is essentially a visible and geographical community, consisting of all those in each locality who profess and call themselves Christians. Other evangelicals stress that the church is a gathered community, consisting only of those who are judged to be born again, and who have subscribed to a full evangelical confession of faith. These two visions of the church are not entirely incompatible, and we should avoid a neat polarization. There are at least two significant convictions which we share.

First, all evangelicals accept the difference between the visible and the invisible church. It becomes especially important when we are thinking and talking about church membership. We agree that God reserves as his prerogative the right to admit people into his true (invisible) church, and he does so when they exercise faith in Christ. But he delegates to pastors the responsibility to admit people by baptism into the visible church, and they do this on the profession of faith.

This distinction leads us to insist that church membership does not guarantee salvation. Paul warns the Corinthians not to imitate the Israelites in the desert. They had all been "baptized into Moses," and had all been partakers of the same spiritual food and drink. In other words, they were the Old Testament equivalent of baptized, communicant members of the church. "Nevertheless, God was not pleased with most of them." Their church membership did not ensure their immunity to his judgment (1 Cor 10:1-5).

Second, all evangelicals regard the purity of the church (doctrinal and ethical) as a proper, God-appointed goal. We differ in our methods of securing it. Some resort to almost Draconian measures, and are quick to excommunicate even mild offenders. Others acknowledge New Testament teaching about church discipline,[10] but they also remember Jesus' parable of the weeds and the wheat, and that "in the visible Church the evil be ever mingled with the good" (*Anglican Article* 26). They are therefore reluctant to resort to excommunication or secession.

It is within this discussion of the purity of the church that a mention of the concept of "comprehensiveness" belongs. The Church of England has been much to blame in boasting of its "glorious comprehensiveness" without recalling that from the beginning a clear distinction was made between "principled" and "unprincipled" comprehensiveness. Bishop J. C. Ryle, in his introduction to *Principles for Churchmen*,[11] lamented the "universal toleration" in the Church of England at the end of the nineteenth century. He wrote with a touch of sarcasm, "What more likely to provide peace and stop quarrelling, than to declare the church a kind of Noah's ark, within which every kind of opinion and creed shall dwell safe and undisturbed, and the only terms of communion shall be willingness to come inside and let your neighbour alone?"[12] The authors of *The Fulness of Christ* (1950) wrote similarly, "There are limits to the principle of comprehension in the Church. . . . The truth of God revealed in Christ may be flexible, but it is not infinitely flexible."[13] Then in 1957 Alec Vidler rejected "an unprincipled syncretism" in favor of "the principle of comprehension" by which "a church ought to hold the fundamentals of the faith and at the same time allow for differences of opinion and of interpretation in secondary matters."[14] In 1973 J. I. Packer clearly distinguished between "the *virtue* of tolerating different views on secondary issues on the basis of clear agreement on essentials" and "the *vice* of retreating from the light of Scripture into an intellectual murk where no outlines are clear, all cats are grey, and syncretism is the prescribed task."[15]

Having reflected on evangelical views of the nature of the church, we are ready now to consider how the Holy Spirit equips the church for her ministry. I begin with the ordained ministry. Evangelicals are agreed from their reading of the New Testament that *episkopē*, pastoral care of some kind, is God's provision for his people. So Paul exhorted the elders of the Ephesian church to keep watch over themselves and over all the flock of which the Holy Spirit had made them overseers (*episkopoi*, Acts 20:28). Thus the Holy Spirit had delegated to them the pastoral care of the church. "Pastors" is therefore the biblically correct name for the leaders of the local church; "priests" is incorrect and misleading. It is never used of them in the New Testament. To be sure, the English word *priest* is harmless because it is only a contraction of the word *presbyter* (meaning "elder"). That is why the Reformers retained the word. But few people can manage the mental gymnastic of saying "priest" while meaning "presbyter." It would be much clearer for all Anglicans to follow the wisdom of the churches of South India, North India and Pakistan, which have a threefold ministry of "bishops, presbyters and deacons." We should also be consistent in all the language we use. Catholic priests may offer a sacrifice on an altar; evangelical pastors serve a supper from a table.

Although in practice some evangelical leaders have been extremely autocratic, in theory they have rejected a clericalism which reserves all ministry to the clergy and denies responsibility to the laity. On the contrary, evangelicals have always believed not only in the priesthood of all believers but in the ministry of all believers as well. And recently, partly through the influence of the charismatic movement, the Pauline vision of the "every-member ministry of the body of Christ" has become widely accepted. Evangelicals are not altogether agreed which of the *charismata* (spiritual gifts) are available today, or which are more important than others. But it should be possible for us to agree (1) that the *nature* of the gifts is varied (some being quite prosaic, like sharing our money and doing acts of mercy); (2) that the *purpose* of the gifts is the common good, to build up the church in both size and depth; and (3) that the *criterion* for evaluating the gifts is the degree to which they build the church. As Paul wrote, "Try to excel in gifts that build up the church" (1 Cor 14:12).

CHRISTIAN MISSION

Mission has always been an evangelical preoccupation, not least the worldwide mission of the church. *Evangelicalism* and *evangelism,* as the words themselves indicate, are inevitably interlocked. And one of our evangelical emphases in evangelism is that the Holy Spirit is the chief evangelist. He is a missionary Spirit, and Pentecost was a missionary event.

John V. Taylor, when he was bishop of Winchester, began his book about the Holy Spirit (*The Go-Between God*) with these words: "The chief actor in the historic mission of the Christian church is the Holy Spirit. He is the director of the whole enterprise."[16] Then the Manila Manifesto, produced during the Second International Congress on World Evangelization in 1989, included this paragraph headed "God the Evangelist":

> The Scriptures declare that God himself is the chief evangelist. For the Spirit of God is the Spirit of truth, love, holiness and power, and evangelism is impossible without him. It is he who anoints the messenger, confirms the word, prepares the hearer, convicts the sinful, enlightens the blind, gives life to the dead, enables us to repent and believe, unites us to the body of Christ, assures us that we are God's children, leads us into Christ-like character and service, and sends us out in our turn to be Christ's witnesses. In all this the Holy Spirit's main preoccupation is to glorify Jesus Christ by showing him to us and forming him in us.[17]

Our Lord Jesus himself, during his ministry on earth, clearly taught the missionary nature of the Holy Spirit, notably in John 7:37-39. It was the last and greatest day of the Feast of Tabernacles. Jesus stood forth in a prominent place in the temple, and said in a loud voice (to emphasize the solemnity of his words):

> "If anyone is thirsty, let him come to me and drink. Whoever believes in me, as the Scripture has said, streams of living water will flow from within him." By this he meant the Spirit, whom those who believed in him were later to receive.

Notice his two distinct references to water—first to drinking water (verse 37, "If anyone is thirsty . . .") and second, to flowing water (verse 38, "streams of living water will flow"). Indeed, the two pictures are fused in a remarkable combination. It is only if we take water into us that it will then flow out from us. When we drink, we take in only small sips. But by the extraordinary operation of the Holy Spirit within us, these sips are transformed into rivers, and drinking-water becomes flowing water. The world is likened to a barren desert, and the Holy Spirit to the irrigation which causes the desert to blossom.

Archbishop William Temple, in his *Readings in St. John's Gospel*, wrote about Jesus' words: "No-one can possess (or rather be indwelt by) the Spirit of God, and keep that Spirit to himself. Where the Spirit is, he flows forth; if there is no flowing forth, he is not there."[18] This link between the Holy Spirit and Christian mission is indissoluble. To neglect mission is to contradict the very being of the Spirit. In consequence, an essential mark of a Spirit-filled church is both its compassionate outreach into its local community and its serious commitment to global mission. Harry Boer expressed this with considerable force:

> When the church tries to bottle up the Spirit within herself, she acts contrary both to her own and to his nature. For it is the nature of the church ever to be enlarging her borders, and it is the nature of the Spirit to transmit his life to ever-widening circles. When the church does not recognise this law of her being and of the being of the Spirit, the Spirit is quenched and he withdraws himself, and the deposit of religiosity that is left becomes a putrefaction in the lives of those who have grieved him.[19]

Before we leave this section on the Holy Spirit and mission, three further aspects of it need to be touched upon.

Evangelism and Social Action

First, there is the question of *evangelism and social action*. This used to be an area of conflict in the evangelical constituency, but seems to be so no longer. The Grand Rapids Report (1982) defined the relationship between the two in the following terms:

1. Social activity is a *consequence* of evangelism, because converts manifest their new life in service.

2. Social activity can be a *bridge* to evangelism, because it often gains a hearing for the gospel.

3. Social activity is a *partner* of evangelism, so that they are "like the two blades of a pair of scissors or the two wings of a bird." As in the public ministry of Jesus, so now words and deeds, proclamation and demonstration, good news and good works go hand in hand.[20]

Evangelism and Miracles

Second, we need to consider *evangelism and miracles*. Should miracles accompany the preaching of the gospel today? During the last decades of the twentieth century a "signs and wonders" movement developed, pioneered specially by the late John Wimber and his Vineyard churches. In his two books *Power Evangelism* (1985) and *Power Healing* (1986) he argued that signs and wonders were "everyday occurrences in New Testament times" and should be in our time too. The theological basis of his reasoning was that, since the kingdom of God was inaugurated by Jesus, and its arrival was demonstrated by his miracles, we should also expect them regularly today.[21] Moreover, some observers have hailed the claimed outbreak of signs and wonders as the "third wave" of the Pentecostal movement in this century. How should we respond to this teaching? To begin with, we should avoid the extreme and opposite reactions of skepticism and credulity.

On the one hand, to deny even the possibility of miracles, whether from theological prejudice or scientific secularism, borders on the absurd. Since we believe that God is the sovereign creator of the universe, he is certainly able to intrude into his own world. We have no liberty either to lock him up in one of our neat little boxes or to dictate to him what he is permitted to do. One of the most brash examples of such unbelief took place in France towards the end of the eighteenth century. Because the Jansenists were claiming that remarkable miracles were being performed at Abbé Paris's tomb, the Roman Catholic authorities first walled up the tomb and then fixed on the wall the peremptory order *De par le roy défense à Dieu de faire miracle en ce lieu* ("By command of the king, God is forbidden to perform miracles here")! "Absurd" is not too strong an epithet for such folly.

At the opposite extreme are those who, in John Wimber's words, regard signs and wonders (especially healing miracles) as characterizing "the normal Christian life."[22] But this cannot be so, for several reasons.

First, whatever our definition of *miracle* may be, it must be the abnorm, not the norm. That is, it is a deviation from God's usual activity. The God of the Bible is primarily the God of nature, not of supernature. He is the God who gives sun and rain, sustains the world, clothes the flowers, feeds the birds, and provides his creatures with life, breath and all things. This is where the biblical revelation of God begins. Miracles neither precede nor supersede it. Their principal purpose in Scripture has been to authenticate each fresh stage of revelation—the law of Moses, the ministry of the prophets from Elijah onward, the teaching of Jesus and the authority of the apostles (e.g., Ex 4:1-9; 1 Kings 17—18; Acts 2:22; 2 Cor 12:12).

In the second place, if (as John Wimber taught) God "has given us the authority to work the works of Jesus,"[23] why should these be limited to healing? Why should we not also multiply loaves and fishes, and so solve the problem of world hunger? And why should we not also be able to still storms, and so rescue people whose lives are threatened by flood?

In the third place, reality does not fit the claims. To promise miraculous healing to all who believe is to cause disillusion, and then to attribute failure to unbelief can only be described as cruel.

To sum up, we should certainly be open to miracle (because God is the Creator), but we have no right to expect miracles with the same frequency with which they occurred in special biblical periods (because ours is not an epoch of revelation). Moreover, we are living in between times, between the "already" of the kingdom inaugurated and the "not yet" of the kingdom consummated. Charismatic and noncharismatic evangelicals should be able to agree with the balanced statement of the Manila Manifesto (1989): "We have no liberty to place limits on the power of the living Creator today. We reject both the scepticism which denies miracles and the presumption which demands them."[24]

Evangelism and Revival

Third, there is the topic of *evangelism and revival.* "A longing for revival," as we saw earlier, is another evangelical characteristic. We talk about it, tend to know about some of the great revivals in church history, and pray for it. So what does it mean? Most evangelicals would agree that revival is an altogether supernatural visitation by the sovereign Spirit of God, so that a whole community becomes aware of and awed by his holy presence.[25] The unconverted are convicted of sin, repent and cry to God for mercy, often in large numbers and without any human agency. Backsliders are restored. The half-hearted are reinvigorated. And all the people of God, overwhelmed with a sense of his majesty, display the ninefold fruit of the Spirit and devote themselves to good works.

CHRISTIAN HOPE

The Old Testament looked forward to the outpouring or gift of the Spirit as the principal, indeed the defining, blessing of the messianic age. The messianic age would be the age of the Spirit. So when the Holy Spirit came in power on the Day of Pentecost, God's expectant people knew that the new age had dawned, and that the kingdom of God had broken into history. They also knew, however, that this coming of the kingdom was only partial; and that a final fulfillment of God's promise was yet to come. So the gift of the Holy Spirit was both the beginning of the end time and the divine assurance that the rest would follow at some future time. It was "both a fulfilment of the promise and the promise of fulfilment."[26] This double perspective is expressed in the New Testament by the use of three metaphors: commercial (two installments of a purchase), agricultural (two stages of a harvest), and social (two courses of a feast).

First, the gift of the Spirit is like the down-payment in a transaction; it is both the first installment and the guarantee that the full purchase money will follow. God has "put his Spirit in our hearts as a deposit [*arrabōn*], guaranteeing what is to come" (2 Cor 1:22; cf. 2 Cor 5:5; Eph 1:14).

Second, the gift of the Spirit is like the reaping of the firstfruits; it is both the beginning of the harvest and the guarantee that the rest will follow (Rom 8:23).

Third, the gift of the Spirit is like the first course of a banquet, sometimes called an "appetizer" or (especially in the United Kingdom) a "starter;" it is both the foretaste and the guarantee that the rest of the meal will follow (Heb 6:4-5).

In each case the Holy Spirit is both gift and promise, both initial experience and future hope. We evangelical Christians do not agree with one another in the details of our eschatology, and we continue to debate questions relating to the tribulation, the rapture and the millennium. But we all believe in the personal, visible and glorious return of Jesus Christ, in the resurrection of our bodies, and in the new heaven and new earth. Moreover, of these future certainties we also believe that the Holy Spirit is God's pledge. We are living "in between times," between the first and second comings of Christ, between kingdom come and kingdom coming, between present reality and future destiny. And it is the Holy Spirit whose indwelling spans the gulf between the "already" and the "not yet." As the apostle Paul expressed it, "We ourselves, who have the firstfruits of the Spirit, groan inwardly as we wait eagerly for our adoption as sons, the redemption of our bodies" (Rom 8:23).

Here are three affirmations. First, "we groan inwardly" because we share in the fallenness of the whole creation. Second, "we have the firstfruits of the Spirit," the divine pledge of our final inheritance. Third, "we wait eagerly" for our bodily redemption. We also "wait for it patiently" (Rom 8:25). All Christians find it difficult to hold these three perspectives together in balance. Some are so preoccupied with future glory, and with the Spirit who guarantees it, that they never groan, never admit the incompleteness of their present salvation. Others groan and wait eagerly for the glory to come but forget that already they have its foretaste in the Spirit. Others are perplexed by the present tension between the Spirit and the pain, and they forget to wait patiently until the tension is resolved.

Moreover, the waiting to which we are called is to be both eager and patient simultaneously. It is another equilibrium hard to maintain. We are neither to wait so eagerly that we lose our patience, nor to wait so patiently (even lethargically) that we lose our expectancy. Rather, both eagerness and patience are to characterize our waiting. Many of our evangelical divisions, not least between charismatics and noncharismatics, it seems to me, are due to our failure to keep the "already" and the "not yet" in balance.

From beginning to end, from our initiation into Christ until his return, the Holy Spirit has a unique and indispensable role to fulfill. Evangelical Christians remain divided in some matters, especially in our precise understanding of the "baptism" of the Spirit and the "gifts" of the Spirit. But we all recognize that the new birth is a birth of the Spirit; that Christian assurance is due to the inner witness of the Spirit; that holiness is the fruit of the Spirit; that the church is the fellowship of the Spirit; that the Christian mission owes its impetus to the Spirit; and that the Christian hope is kindled by the gift of the Spirit, who is the first installment of our final inheritance.

We are immensely privileged that the Lord Jesus, who was born and died for us, who was raised from the dead and exalted to the Father, then sent his Spirit to live and work in us. The Christian life is life in the Spirit. Without his indwelling presence and power it would be both inconceivable and impossible. In this evangelical Christians are agreed.

Suggested Further Reading

Alexander, Donald L., ed. *Christian Spirituality.* Downers Grove, Ill.: InterVarsity Press, 1988.

Graham, Billy. *The Holy Spirit.* Rev. ed. Dallas: Word, 1988.

Green, Michael. *I Believe in the Holy Spirit.* Rev. ed. Grand Rapids: Eerdmans, 1989.

Pinnock, Clark. *Flame of Love.* Downers Grove, Ill.: InterVarsity Press, 1996.

Sproul, R. C. *The Mystery of the Holy Spirit.* Wheaton, Ill.: Tyndale House, 1994.

Wells, David F. *God the Evangelist: How the Holy Spirit Works to Bring Men and Women to Faith.* Grand Rapids: Eerdmans, 1999.

Conclusion
The Challenge of the Evangelical Faith

WE HAVE BEEN PREOCCUPIED THROUGHOUT MUCH of this book with the trinitarian shape of the evangelical faith, that is, with the initiative of God in revealing himself, the love of Christ in dying for our sins, and the ministry of the Holy Spirit in facilitating every aspect of our Christian discipleship. More simply, we have focused on the Word, the cross and the Spirit as three essential evangelical emphases. To be an evangelical Christian, however, is not just to subscribe to an orthodox trinitarian formula. The evangelical faith reaches beyond belief to behavior; it brings with it a multifaceted challenge to live accordingly.

An outstanding example of this was given by the apostle Paul at the end of the first chapter of his Philippian letter. He refers to "the gospel of Christ" and to "the faith of the gospel" (Phil 1:27), that is, to the evangelical faith, and he begs his readers to live appropriately.

> Whatever happens, conduct yourselves in a manner worthy of the gospel
> of Christ. Then, whether I come and see you or only hear about you in
> my absence, I will know that you stand firm in one spirit, contending as
> one man for the faith of the gospel without being frightened in any way
> by those who oppose you. This is a sign to them that they will be de-

stroyed, but that you will be saved—and that by God. For it has been granted to you on behalf of Christ not only to believe on him, but also to suffer for him, since you are going through the same struggle you saw I had, and now hear that I still have. (Phil 1:27-30)

There is something profoundly moving about this appeal. The apostle is a prisoner, either in Rome (as traditionally thought) or in Ephesus (as some hold). In either case he is under house arrest, his liberty is curtailed, and he is unable either to visit the churches he has planted or to engage in more pioneer evangelism. Moreover, his future is full of uncertainty. He realizes that he may be approaching death. Indeed, he feels torn between life and death. His personal desire is "to depart and be with Christ, which is better by far." The churches still need him, however, so he is fairly sure he will be released and will resume his apostolic labor. Yet beyond both options he longs for the glory of Christ: "so that now as always Christ will be exalted in my body, whether by life or by death" (Phil 1:20-26).

"Whatever happens," he continues (Phil 1:27), that is, whether he lives or dies, his principal concern is not what will happen to him but what will happen to the gospel; not for himself and his personal survival but for the survival and spread of the gospel. It is in the light of this concern that he issues to the Philippians (and so to us) a stirring fivefold summons.

EVANGELICAL INTEGRITY, OR A LIFE
WORTHY OF THE GOSPEL

The verb *politeuomai*, which occurs only twice in the New Testament, meant originally to live as the citizen (*politēs*) of a city-state (*polis*). Paul may have chosen the word because Philippi was a Roman colony (as Luke correctly stated in Acts 16:12), and its inhabitants as Roman citizens had special privileges and responsibilities. The Christians in Philippi must therefore ensure that their manner of life as citizens was worthy of the gospel. But Paul is surely also referring to their heavenly citizenship. "Our citizenship is in heaven," he will remind them in Philippians 3:20. This gave them even greater privileges and higher responsibilities.

Christians are, in fact, the citizens of two kingdoms. An anonymous defense of Christianity dating from the middle of the second century, known as *The Letter to Diognetus*, expressed well this paradox of the Christian life, namely our dual citizenship:

> Christians are not distinguished from the rest of humanity by country, language or custom. . . . But while they live in both Greek and barbarian cities . . . and follow the local customs in dress and food and other aspects of life, at the same time they demonstrate the remarkable and admittedly unusual character of their own citizenship. They live in their own countries, but only as aliens; they participate in everything as citizens, and endure everything as foreigners. . . . They live on earth, but their citizenship is in heaven. . . . In a word, what the soul is to the body, Christians are to the world.[1]

I have characterized this first summons as the call for evangelical integrity because the concept of living a life that is "worthy" expresses not merit but correspondence. Our conduct is to be in keeping with our calling (Eph 4:1), our repentance (Lk 3:8), our Lord (Mt 10:37), and the God who calls us into his kingdom and glory (Col 1:10; 1 Thess 2:12). There is to be no dichotomy between what we profess and what we practice, between what we say and what we are, but rather a fundamental consistency. The alternative is set before us with great plainness of speech in Paul's letter to Titus. On the one hand, inconsistent Christian conduct gives people cause to "malign the word of God" and so hinders evangelism. On the other hand, consistent Christian conduct "will make the teaching about God our Savior attractive" and so will promote evangelism (Tit 2:5, 10). More briefly, bad behavior discredits the gospel, while good behavior adorns and so commends it.

Our evangelical forebears went in hot pursuit of what they called "scriptural" or "practical" holiness. They took with great seriousness the frequently repeated command of God to his covenant people "Be holy, because I am holy." Today, however, some evangelical people seem to acquiesce in moral standards that are indistinguishable from those of the world. Others have allowed the quest for holiness to be displaced by the search for social justice or for religious experience. These things are important, but not at the expense of the hunger and thirst for righteousness.

EVANGELICAL STABILITY, OR STANDING FIRM IN THE GOSPEL

"Then, whether I come and see you or only hear about you in my absence, I will know that you stand firm in one spirit" (Phil 1:27). Before considering this reference to unity we will concentrate on the call to stability, for it was this which concerned Paul most. He longed to know (whether by sight or by hearsay) that they were standing firm.

Stability is important in every sphere. We talk about the need for a stable government and a stable economy, about stable buildings and stable characters. And Christian stability obviously meant much to the apostles. Luke tells us, they revisited the cities they had evangelized, "strengthening" or establishing the converts (Acts 18:23). They knew the strength of satanic opposition—intellectual (false teaching), moral (temptation) and physical (persecution). Yet God's ability to "establish" his people was a vital ingredient of Paul's gospel (Rom 16:25). So he exhorted them to stand firm. He used the same verb in relation to Christian soldiers, who were to fight against the principalities and powers of evil, to put on the armor of God, and so (four times in Eph 6:10-17) to "stand."

Yet stability in both doctrine and ethics is in short supply today. Instead, we seem like fragile boats in an ocean storm, "tossed about by the waves and whirled around by every fresh gust of teaching" (Eph 4:14 REB). It is much easier to drift with the stream than to swim against it.

It takes much less effort to bend like reeds, shaken by the winds of public opinion and political correctness, than to stand firm and immovable like rocks in a mountain torrent. The call to evangelical stability is much needed today. Its chief foundation is the rock of Holy Scripture, that is, of evangelical truth, to which we now turn.

EVANGELICAL TRUTH, OR CONTENDING FOR THE FAITH OF THE GOSPEL

Evidently we are not only to stand firm in the gospel ourselves, but to fight for it in the public arena as well. "Contending for the gospel" might be described as a combination of evangelism and apologetics. It is not enough to proclaim the good news; we have also to defend it and confirm it (Phil 1:7, 16). The apostles did not separate these tasks. There was a strong element of apologetics in all their evangelism. The apostle Paul could even sum up his ministry by two Greek words which can be translated "we persuade people" (cf. 2 Cor 5:11). And Luke describes him doing so—arguing the gospel, reasoning with people out of the Scriptures and convincing them of its truth.

The contemporary church needs to follow the apostolic example. We must be able to say what Paul said to the procurator Festus: "I am not insane, most excellent Festus. . . . What I am saying is true and reasonable" (Acts 26:25). Moreover, we should never set arguments and the Holy Spirit over against each other, declaring that if we are really trusting the Holy Spirit we will not need arguments, or as we do develop arguments, placing our trust plainly in them, not in him. This is a grievously false antithesis. The Holy Spirit is the Spirit of truth, who cares about the truth, teaches the truth and bears witness to the truth. Consequently, truth and the Holy Spirit are entirely compatible, and it is perfectly possible to trust both simultaneously. He brings people to faith in Jesus Christ *through* our words and arguments when he enlightens their minds to perceive the truth and feel the force of our own message.

Evangelical Unity, or Working Together for the Gospel

Unity is one of the main themes of Paul's letter to the Philippians. There seems to have been some serious discord in the church. We are not told why, but there may be a clue in the three notable conversions which took place during Paul's missionary visit (Acts 16:11ff.).

It would be hard to imagine a more disparate trio, differing from each other nationally and socially, and perhaps temperamentally as well. Lydia was a wealthy businesswoman from the province of Asia; the anonymous slave girl came from the opposite end of the social spectrum; while the Roman jailer, probably a retired soldier, might be described as belonging to the respectable middle class. These were three foundational members of the Philippian church. It is wonderful that they could have been welcomed by baptism into the Christian community without any discrimination. Perhaps there were other converts from similarly different backgrounds. Is it possible that the old tensions of race, class and personality resurfaced after their conversion and caused some conflict?

At all events we note the apostle's exhortations. He begs his readers to "stand firm in one spirit, contending as one man for the faith of the gospel" (Phil 1:27). He goes on, urging them to "make my joy complete by being like-minded, having the same love, being one in spirit and purpose" (Phil 2:2). It is important to observe, however, what kind of unity Paul is commending. It is neither unity at any price, even compromising fundamental truths in order to attain it, nor unity in every particular, separating from anybody who fails to dot every "I" and cross every "t" as we do. It is rather unity in the gospel, in evangelical essentials, "standing . . . side by side in the struggle to advance the gospel faith" (Phil 1:27 REB).

Today, however, many of us evangelical Christians acquiesce too readily in our pathological tendency to fragment. We take refuge in our conviction about the invisible unity of the church, as if its visible manifestation did not matter. In consequence, the devil has been hugely successful in his old strategy to divide and conquer. Our disunity remains a major hindrance to our evangelism. In particular, we need a greater measure of discernment, so that we may distinguish between evangelical essentials which cannot be compromised and those *adiaphora* ('matters indifferent') on which, being of secondary importance, it is not necessary for us to insist. Perhaps our criterion for deciding which is which should be as follows.

Whenever different conclusions are reached by equally biblical Christians who are equally anxious to understand the teaching of Scripture and to submit to its authority, we should deduce that evidently Scripture is not crystal clear in this matter, and therefore we can afford to give one another liberty. We can also hope—through prayer, study and discussion—to grow in our understanding and so in our agreement.

What could be regarded today as belonging to the category of the *adiaphora*? A long list could be compiled. Here are twelve suggestions. I will frame them as questions.[2]

1. *Baptism.* Should we baptize only adult believers or their infants as well? And by immersion or affusion?

2. *The Lord's Supper.* How should we define our sharing in the body and blood of Christ (1 Cor 10:16)?

3. *Church government.* Should it be episcopal, presbyterian or congregationalist?

4. *Worship.* Is there a place for liturgy, or should all public prayer be *ex tempore*? Can we combine the formal and the informal?

5. *Charismata.* Are any not available today? And of those which are, which are the most important?

6. *Women.* Are all ministries open to them or does Scripture preclude certain functions? What does masculine "headship" mean, and how does it apply today?

7. *Ecumenism.* What degree of involvement with nonevangelical churches is appropriate?

8. *Old Testament prophecy.* How are we to understand its fulfillment?

9. *Sanctification.* What degree of holiness is possible for the people of God on earth?

10. *The state.* What should be the relations between church and state?

11. *Mission.* Are "mission" and "evangelism" synonymous? What is the place of the quest for social justice?

12. *Eschatology.* How do we understand the tribulation, the rapture, the millennium, the parousia and our final destinies?

This list could be considerably extended. It should include all doctrines and practices in which there is a sincere disagreement among evangelical believers about what the Bible teaches or implies. But these secondary matters, in which we can afford to give each other freedom of conscience, leave primary Christian truths intact, especially those which relate to the person and work of Christ, as defined in the Apostles' Creed and the Nicene Creed, together with the great Reformation emphases on the supreme authority of Scripture, the atoning death of Christ, the justification of sinners by grace alone through faith alone, and the indispensable ministry of the Holy Spirit. On these we must insist. For according to the apostles, to deny the divine-human person of Jesus Christ is anti-Christ (1 Jn 2:18ff.; 4:1ff.) and to deny the gospel of free grace is to deserve the judgment of God (Gal 1:6ff.).

This combination of unity in the primary truths and freedom in the secondary, while preserving love in all situations, is often summarized in proverbial form; for instance, "In truth unity, in doubtful matters liberty, in all things charity." This epigram is sometimes (though inaccurately) attributed to Augustine, but its true author seems to have been Rupert Meldenius—whose name turns out to be an anagram of Petrus Meuderlin, a Latinized form of seventeenth-century Lutheran theologian Peter Meiderlin. In a Latin treatise (c. 1620) which defended Lutheranism but pleaded for peace, he wrote, "If we would but observe 'unity in essentials, liberty in non-essentials, charity in all things,' our affairs would certainly be in the best possible situation."

In the English-speaking world, however, it was the great Puritan Richard Baxter who popularized the proverb by quoting it in his book *The Reformed Pastor* (1656). It is said to have been his favorite quotation.[3] It could profitably be ours as well. It would help us to develop the "culture of civility" for which Alister McGrath pleads within evangelicalism. "Can we give up our personality cults," he asks, "petty rivalries, historical feuds and personal agendas for the greater good of the movement?"[4] I hope we can answer his question in the affirmative.

EVANGELICAL ENDURANCE, OR SUFFERING FOR THE GOSPEL

Paul's summons to the Philippians to "contend" for the gospel faith implies the existence of adversaries. To these he now comes. He exhorts his readers, as they battle for the truth, not to be in any way "frightened" by their opponents. The apostle uses a strong term "unique in the Greek Bible and denoting the uncontrollable stampede of startled horses."[5] The Philippian experience of opposition to the gospel, together with their refusal to be intimidated by it, would convey a double message. It would be a clear sign from God to their opponents "that they will be destroyed" but to them that they "will be saved" (Phil 1:28) for, Paul further explains, the Philippian Christians had been granted on behalf of Christ two privileges, "not only to believe on him, but also to suffer for him" (Phil 1:29) He is not referring to pain and suffering in general but in particular to suffering for the gospel.

It is truly remarkable that faith and suffering (faith in Christ and suffering for Christ) should be bracketed in this way as two gifts of God's grace. Of course all Christians are believers, but are they also all called to suffer? And can suffering be regarded as being as much a gift or privilege as is faith? Yes, this is the consistent teaching of the New Testament.

Each of Jesus' eight Beatitudes, which began his Sermon on the Mount, depicts a different characteristic of the citizens of God's kingdom, so that the eight together portray a rounded Christian disciple. The eighth pronounces God's blessing on those "who are persecuted because of righteousness" (Mt 5:10ff.; cf. Jn 15:18ff.). So the early Christians were not surprised by the opposition they experienced. Instead they rejoiced "because they had been counted worthy of suffering disgrace for the Name" (Acts 5:41). Paul wrote that "everyone who wants to live a godly life in Christ Jesus will be persecuted" (2 Tim 3:12), while Peter declared suffering to be a part of the Christian calling and told his readers to rejoice that they were privileged to share in Christ's sufferings (1 Pet 2:21; 4:13). No wonder then that Paul saw the Philippians as "going through the same struggle" which they had seen him experience in Philippi (flogging, imprisonment and the stocks), and which they now heard he was still experiencing (verse 30). Disciples are called to share their Master's sufferings, and also the sufferings of the apostles. It is an inevitable aspect of the apostolic succession—a succession not of order or even of doctrine or mission but of suffering.

This noble succession, moreover, reaches down to the present day. Those of us who live in the West may not be called upon to suffer much or physically, although faithfulness to the gospel, because it undermines human pride and selfishness, always arouses opposition. But in other parts of the world there is much physical persecution for truth and righteousness. Indeed, it is reliably calculated that the number of Christian martyrs was greater in the twentieth century than in any previous period of church history.

It was appropriate, therefore, that the ten niches above the west door of Westminster Abbey in London, which had been vacant for more than five hundred years, in July 1998 were filled with the statues of twentieth-century Christian martyrs representing different denominations and every continent. These include well-known names like Dietrich Bonhoeffer (victim of Nazi tyranny), Martin Luther King Jr. (civil rights campaigner) and Archbishop Janani Luwum (assassinated by Ugandan dictator Idi Amin), but also comparatively unknown martyrs like Esther John, a Pakistani convert from Islam who was brutally murdered in her bed, and Wang Zhiming, a Chinese pastor who was publicly executed during the cultural revolution.[6] To each martyr Jesus surely said, "Be faithful, even to the point of death, and I will give you the crown of life" (Rev 2:10).

We can hardly fail to be stirred by the apostle's summons at the end of Philippians 1 as it comes to us across the centuries. He calls us to live a life that is worthy of the gospel, to stand firm in it, to contend for it earnestly, to struggle for it together and to be willing to suffer for it. All this is involved in the challenge to maintain the evangelical faith today.

SUGGESTED FURTHER READING

Boice, James Montgomery. *Foundations of God's City.* Downers Grove, Ill.: InterVarsity Press, 1999.

Bonhoeffer, Dietrich. *The Cost of Discipleship.* London: SCM Press, 1959.

Borthwick, Paul. *Six Dangerous Questions.* Downers Grove, Ill.: InterVarsity Press, 1996.

Colson, Charles. *The Burden of Truth.* Wheaton, Ill.: Tyndale House, 1998.

McGrath, Alister. *"I Believe": Exploring the Apostles' Creed.* Downers Grove, Ill.: InterVarsity Press, 1997.

Sire, James W. *Discipleship of the Mind.* Downers Grove, Ill.: InterVarsity Press, 1990.

Postscript
The Preeminence of Humility

I MAKE SO BOLD AS TO CLAIM, IN THIS BRIEF POSTSCRIPT, that the supreme quality which the evangelical faith engenders (or should do) is humility.

Already I think I can see the wry smile on my readers' faces, for we have to confess that our reputation is very different. Evangelical people are often regarded as proud, vain, arrogant and cocksure. What I mean, however, is that the principal tenets which evangelical Christians cherish, if they are correctly understood, inevitably tend towards humility. As Thomas Cranmer's *Homily on Salvation* put it, evangelical convictions set forth the true glory of God and are bound therefore to beat down the vainglory of human beings.

Let me explain further. I have been at pains to argue that evangelical Christianity is trinitarian Christianity. We hold the three "Rs"—revelation, redemption and regeneration, associating revelation with the Father, redemption with the Son and regeneration with the Holy Spirit. We desire above all else to bear witness to the supreme authority of the Word of God, the atoning efficacy of the cross of Christ and the indispensable ministries of the Holy Spirit.

Yet the more the three persons of the Trinity are glorified, the more completely human pride is excluded. To magnify the self-revelation of God is to confess our complete ignorance without it. To magnify the cross of Christ is to confess our utter lostness without it. To magnify the regenerating, indwelling and sanctifying role of the Holy Spirit is to confess our abiding self-centeredness without it. The Word, the cross and the Spirit, as we have seen, have a special place of honor in our thinking. We kneel before God the Father with the Bible open before us emphatically not because we are bibliolaters but because we desire humbly to hear God's word. We kneel in imagination at the feet of the crucified and resurrected Lord (as when we come to the Communion table) because we desire humbly to receive that full and free forgiveness which only he can give. We kneel also before the Holy Spirit because we desire humbly to ask him to fill our emptiness and to cause his fruit to ripen in our lives.

Without the Bible we would grope and stagger in thick darkness. Without the cross we would flounder in the deep waters of guilt and alienation, with no mercy, no redemption, no forgiveness and no hope. Without the indwelling Spirit we would be the helpless victims of indwelling sin, of pathetic self-effort and so of unremitting failure. It is in this way that we understand why Jesus gave us the model of a child's humility.

> At that time the disciples came to Jesus and asked, "Who is the greatest in the kingdom of heaven?" He called a little child and had him stand among them. And he said: "I tell you the truth, unless you change and become like little children, you will never enter the kingdom of heaven. Therefore, whoever humbles himself like this child is the greatest in the kingdom of heaven." (Mt 18:1-4)

Many people are perplexed by Jesus' references to the "humility" of a child. In our experience children are usually headstrong and proud. So Jesus was alluding not to the character or conduct of children but their status. Everything children possess they have been given, and everything they know they have been taught. It is right therefore to call them "dependents." Just as children depend totally on their parents, so we depend on God, not least in the three spheres mentioned.

On one occasion Jesus said, "I praise you, Father, Lord of heaven and earth, because you have hidden these things from the wise and learned, and revealed them to little children" (Mt 11:25). This is not obscurantism. It is rather to acknowledge that God hides from the intellectually arrogant and reveals himself only to "babies" (as the word here means), that is, to those who are sincere and humble in their approach.

On another occasion, when Jesus invited children to come to him, he added that "anyone who will not receive the kingdom of God like a little child will never enter it" (Mk 10:13-16). Thus the kingdom of God, a synonym in Jesus' teaching for salvation or eternal life, could not be earned or deserved. It could only be "received," as a child receives a gift, freely and gratefully—not like an adult who proudly insists on paying for it.

In the case of our third dependency, namely for holiness, Jesus did not use the simile of the child, but he taught the same truth differently. In developing his allegory of the vine he said, "Apart from me you can do nothing" (Jn 15:5). This "nothing" cannot be interpreted as an absolute, for people can do many things without abiding in Christ or relying on the Holy Spirit. Unregenerate people get up, wash and dress, have their breakfast and go to work without any conscious dependence on Christ or his Spirit. His "nothing" must therefore be interpreted in relation to its context of "fruitfulness." It is logically impossible to bear the fruit of the Spirit if we are not indwelt by the Spirit whose fruit it is.

There is here a fundamental conflict between liberal and evangelical Christianity. During the 1960s, under the influence of extreme liberals like Bishop John Robinson in the United Kingdom and Paul van Buren in the United States, a so-called secular theology was born that proclaimed "Man has come of age" and can therefore dispense with the traditional notions of God and of salvation. But it is impossible to reconcile this call to independence with Jesus' teaching about our dependence on God, Father, Son and Holy Spirit. At least in our Christian hymnody, if

not always in our theology, we express our humble dependence on the
Trinity. Our dependence on God and his Word:

> Word of the ever-living God,
> Will of his glorious Son,
> Without thee how could earth be trod
> Or heaven itself be won?
> Lord, grant that we aright may learn
> The wisdom it imparts,
> And to its heavenly teaching turn
> With simple, childlike hearts.
> (Bernard Barton, 1784-1849)

Our dependence on Christ and his cross:

> Nothing in my hand I bring;
> Simply to thy cross I cling;
> Naked, come to thee for dress;
> Helpless, look to thee for grace;
> Foul, I to the fountain fly,
> Wash me, Saviour, or I die.
> (Augustus M. Toplady, 1740-1778)

Our dependence on the Holy Spirit and his work:

> And every virtue we possess,
> And every victory won,
> And every thought of holiness
> Are his alone.
> Spirit of purity and grace,
> Our weakness, pitying, see;
> O make our hearts thy dwelling-place,
> And worthier thee.
> (Harriet Auber, 1773-1862)

Worship on earth anticipates worship in heaven. For throughout eternity the redeemed will attribute their salvation to him who sits on the throne and to the Lamb. There is no place for human boasting. "Let him who boasts boast in the Lord" (1 Cor 1:31). Our place is on our faces, prostrate before God, and our only appropriate anthem is the Gloria:

> Glory be to the Father, and to the Son, and to the Holy Spirit. As it was in the beginning, is now, and ever shall be, world without end. Amen.

Notes

Preface

[1]Mark Twain, *The Adventures of Tom Sawyer* (1876; New York: Penguin, 1986), p. 37.

[2]From the epilogue to A. M. Ramsey, *From Gore to Temple 1889-1939* (London: Longmans, 1960), p. 166.

[3]John Habgood, *Confessions of a Conservative Liberal* (London: SPCK, 1988), pp. 2-3.

[4]S. C. Neill, *Anglicanism* (1958; New York: Penguin, 1982), p. 190.

[5]Marcus Loane, from his 1980 presidential address to the Sydney Synod.

Introduction: Evangelical Essentials

[1]Patrick Johnstone, *Operation World* (Grand Rapids: Zondervan, 1995), p. 35.

[2]John S. Peart-Binns, *Wand of London* (London: Mowbray, 1987), p. 29.

[3]Michael Saward, *Evangelicals on the Move* (London: Mowbray, 1987), p. 1.

[4]David Hare, *Racing Demon* (London: Faber, 1990), p. 59.

[5]James Davison Hunter, *Culture Wars* (New York: BasicBooks, 1991), p. 144.

[6]Martin Luther, *A Commentary on St. Paul's Epistle to the Galatians* (Cambridge: James Clarke, 1953), p. 53.

[7]Hugh Latimer, *The Works of Hugh Latimer* (Cambridge: Cambridge University Press, 1844-1845), 1:30-31.

[8]John Jewel, *The Works of John Jewel* (Cambridge: Cambridge University Press, 1845-1850), 2:1034.

[9]John Wesley, *The Character of a Methodist* (1742), p. 10.

[10]Billy Graham, *Just As I Am* (Grand Rapids: Zondervan, 1997), p. 160.

[11]Carl F. H. Henry, *The Uneasy Conscience of Modern Fundamentalism* (Grand Rapids: Eerdmans, 1947), p. 26.

[12]See James Barr, *Fundamentalism* (London: SCM Press, 1966), and John Shelby Spong, *Rescuing the Bible from Fundamentalism* (New York: Harper, 1991). Harriet A. Harries considers James Barr's critique valid, and she develops it. She distinguishes three meanings of the word *fundamentalism*: (1) "a historical movement of the 1920s" (in opposition, that is, to "modernism"), (2) "an identity still assumed by old-style separatist fundamentalists, politicized neo-fundamentalists and occasionally also by evangelicals," and (3) "a mentality which has affected much of mainstream evangelicalism" (*Fundamentalism and Evangelicals* [Oxford: Oxford University Press, 1998], p. 313). It is clearly important to distinguish between the history, the identity and the mentality, and Harriet Harries's thorough study deserves careful evaluation. But evangelicals will resist the continuing attempt to identify them with fundamentalists or

to accuse them of having "a rationalistic, fundamentalist mind-set" (e.g., pp. 11-15).

[13]Henry, *Uneasy Conscience,* pp. 36-37.

[14]Rowland Croucher, *Recent Trends Among Evangelicals* (n.p.: Albatross-Marc, 1986), p. 7.

[15]Clive Calver and Rob Warner, *Together We Stand* (London: Hodder & Stoughton, 1996), pp. 128-30.

[16]Peter Beyerhaus, "Lausanne Between Berlin and Geneva," in *Reich Gottes oder Weltgemein-schaft,* ed. W. Künneth and P. Beyerhaus (Liebenzell: Verlag der Liebenzeller Mission, 1975), pp. 307-8.

[17]J. I. Packer, *The Evangelical Anglican Identity Problem: An Analysis* (Oxford: Latimer House, 1978), pp. 15-23. Alister McGrath adopted and expounded these six "fundamental" or "controlling" principles in his book *Evangelicalism and the Future of Christianity* (Downers Grove, Ill.: InterVarsity Press, 1994), pp. 49-88.

[18]D. W. Bebbington, *Evangelicalism in Modern Britain: A History from the 1930s to the 1980s* (Boston: Unwin Hyman, 1989), p. 3. Bebbington elaborates these four characteristics, with many historical examples, on pp. 3-19. They have been widely accepted. Clive Calver and Rob Warner adopted them in their book *Together We Stand,* although Rob Warner added two further characteristics, namely "Christocentric" and "longing for revival" (see pp. 94-105). Bebbington's quadrilateral is also quoted by John Martin in *Gospel People?* (London: SPCK, 1997), pp. 9, 13, although he changed the order and added "the search for holiness."

[19]Derek J. Tidball, *Who Are the Evangelicals?* (London: Marshall Pickering, 1994), p. 14.

[20]Bebbington, *Evangelicalism in Modern Britain,* p. 276.

[21]Ibid., p. 4.

[22]In *The Radical Evangelical: Seeking a Place to Stand* (London: SPCK, 1996), Nigel Wright also writes of the primacy of the Trinity in evangelical religion.

Chapter 1: The Revelation of God

[1]Quoted by D. W. Bebbington, *Evangelicalism in Modern Britain: A History from the 1930s to the 1980s* (Boston: Unwin Hyman, 1989), p. 86.

[2]Alec Motyer, *Look to the Rock: An Old Testament Background to our Understanding of Christ* (Leicester, England: Inter-Varsity Press, 1996), p. 182.

[3]Diogenes Allen, *Christian Belief in a Post-modern World: The Full Wealth of Conviction* (Louisville, Ky.: Westminster John Knox, 1989), pp. 1-9. Several other books published in the 1990s have examined the interaction between evangelicalism and postmodernism. Among them are Stanley J. Grenz, *Revisioning Evangelical Theology: A Fresh Agenda for the 21st Century* (Downers Grove, Ill.: InterVarsity Press, 1993); Dave Tomlinson, *The Post-Evangelical* (London: SPCK, 1995); J. Richard Middleton and Brian J. Walsh, *Truth Is Stranger Than It Used to Be: Biblical Faith in a Postmodern Age* (Downers Grove, Ill.: InterVarsity Press, 1995); and David Hilborn, *Picking Up the Pieces: Can Evangelicals Adapt to Contemporary Culture?* (London: Hodder & Stoughton, 1997). Millard J. Erickson (*The Evangelical Left: Encountering Post-conservative Evangelical Theology* [Grand Rapids, Mich.: Baker, 1997]) offers a fair evaluation, both positive and negative, of North American "postconservatives."

[4]Os Guinness, *Fit Bodies, Fat Minds: Why Evangelicals Don't Think and What to Do About It* (Grand Rapids: Baker, 1994), p. 105.

[5]Peter Cotterell in *The London Bible College Review* (1989).

[6]Some modern versions read that "all inspired Scripture is useful," implying that some Scripture is not inspired and therefore not useful. But (1) the concept of "uninspired Scripture" would have been a contradiction in terms, and (2) the inclusion in the Greek text of *kai* ("and") indicates that Paul is making two statements: that Scripture is God-breathed; and that it is useful. The essay by B. B. Warfield on the "expiration" of Scripture and on the meaning and implications of this text has never been either bettered or refuted. See his *The Inspiration and Authority of the Bible* (Phillipsburg, N.J.: Presbyterian & Reformed, 1951), chap. 3.

[7]J. I. Packer, *"Fundamentalism" and the Word of God* (Leicester, England: Inter-Varsity Christian Fellowship, 1958), pp. 81-82. Packer supplies the references.

[8]Ibid., p. 81.

[9]Ibid., p. 82.

[10]Richard Hooker, *Laws of Ecclesiastical Polity* (1593-1597), 5.8.11.

[11]Note that in the six antitheses of the Sermon on the Mount, "You have heard that it was said . . . but I say to you," Jesus was not contradicting what was "written" (Scripture) but what was "said" (oral tradition).

[12]*The Lambeth Conference* (London: SPCK, 1958), part 2, p. 5.

[13]Alister McGrath, *To Know and Serve God: A Biography of J. I. Packer* (London: Hodder & Stoughton, 1997), pp. 201-2.

[14]Kenneth S. Kantzer and Carl F. H. Henry, eds., *Evangelical Affirmations* (Grand Rapids: Zondervan/Academie, 1990), pp. 32, 38.

[15]E. D. Hirsch, *Validity in Interpretation* (New Haven, Conn.: Yale University Press, 1967), p. 1.

[16]Ibid., p. 5.

[17]John Stott, ed., *Making Christ Known: Historic Mission Documents from the Lausanne Movement 1974-1989* (London: Paternoster, 1997), pp. 13-14. The Chicago Statement on Biblical Inerrancy (1978) elaborated the Lausanne Covenant clause, saying that Scripture "is to be believed as God's instruction in all that it affirms; obeyed as God's command in all that it requires; and embraced as God's pledge in all that it promises."

Chapter 2: The Cross of Christ

[1]J. C. Ryle, *Home Truths* (Thynne, n.d.), pp. 19-20.

[2]P. T. Forsyth, *The Cruciality of the Cross* (London: Hodder & Stoughton, 1909), pp. 44-45.

[3]P. T. Forsyth, *The Work of Christ* (London: Hodder & Stoughton, 1910), p. 53.

[4]Leon Morris, *The Cross in the New Testament* (London: Paternoster, 1965), p. 365.

[5]Ryle, *Home Truths*, p. 4.

[6]E. S. Abbott et al., *Catholicity: A Study in the Conflict of Christian Traditions in the West* (Westminster: Dacre Press, 1947).

[7]Ibid., pp. 21-23.

[8]*The Fulness of Christ: The Church's Growth into Catholicity* (London: SPCK, 1950), pp. 17, 23.

[9]Dag Hammarskjöld, *Markings* (London: Faber, 1964), esp. pp. 128-29.

[10]Charles Smyth, *Cyril Forster Garbett, Archbishop of York* (London: Hodder & Stoughton, 1959), p. 424.

[11]Hilton C. Oswald, ed., *Luther's Works* (St. Louis: Concordia, 1972), 25:291, 345.

[12]Emil Brunner, *The Mediator* (Philadelphia: Westminster Press, 1947), p. 141.

[13]Emil Brunner, *Man in Revolt* (1937; ET London: Lutterworth, 1939), p. 129.

[14]Emil Brunner, *Dogmatics*, trans. Olive Wyon (Philadelphia: Westminster Press, 1950-1979), 2:92-93.

[15]Swami Vivekananda, *Speeches and Writings*, 3rd ed. (Madras: G. A. Natesan, 1893), pp. 38-39.

[16]Ibid., p. 125.

[17]Alister McGrath, *To Know and Serve God: A Biography of James I. Packer* (London: Hodder & Stoughton, 1997), p. 205.

[18]Martin Luther, *Commentary on the Epistle to the Galatians* (1535; Cambridge: James Clarke, 1953), p. 143, cf. p. 101.

[19]Thomas Cranmer, *First Book of Homilies* (1547), in *Homilies and Canons* (London: SPCK, 1914), pp. 25-26.

[20]R. T. Beckwith, G. E. Duffield and J. I. Packer, *Across the Divide* (Abingdon: Marcham Manor Press, 1977), p. 58. It is true that other contemporary scholars challenge both the centrality of justification in Paul's theology and its traditional interpretation which, they suggest, owes more to Luther's dramatic experience than to New Testament teaching. See, for example, Tom Wright, *What St Paul Really Said* (London: Lion, 1997). Certainly we agree that justification is only one Pauline metaphor of atonement and salvation. But I have not myself been convinced by this "new perspective on Paul." We must surely hold on to the truth that justification is a gift of God's grace, which on account of the cross is free and undeserved (e.g., Rom 3:24; 5:15-17; 6:23).

[21]From Richard Hooker's "Definition of Justification," chap. 33 of his *Ecclesiastical Polity* (1593-1597).

[22]Dietrich Bonhoeffer, *The Cost of Discipleship* (1937), pp. 8, 73.

[23]William Temple, *Nature, Man and God* (London: Macmillan, 1934), p. 401.

[24]Alfred Ayer, *The Guardian Weekly*, August 30, 1979.

Chapter 3: The Ministry of the Holy Spirit

[1]Council of Trent 7.8.

[2]Richard Hooker *Ecclesiastical Polity* 5.67.

[3]James Ussher, *The Body of Divinity* (London: Tho. Downes and Geo. Badger, 1649), chap. 42.

[4]J. C. Ryle, *Knots Untied* (1877; Thynne "people's edition," 1900), p. 6.

[5]It is because of our doctrine of assurance that evangelicals have always opposed the practice of praying for the Christian departed. Of course we continue to remember them; it would be very odd, not to say inhuman, to allow death suddenly to erase them from our memory. And we also thank God for them. Why then do we not pray for them? For two reasons. First, although on innumerable occasions in the New Testament we are exhorted to pray for the living, there is no single New Testament text which bids us pray for the dead. So the practice lacks biblical warrant. Second, we are assured that having been justified by faith, "we have peace with God through our Lord Jesus Christ" (Rom 5:1). In addition, Paul told the Colossians to give thanks to the Father "who has qualified you to share in the inheritance of the saints in the kingdom of light" (Col 1:12-14). How then can we pray (using the traditional

phraseology) that the souls of the departed may "rest in peace" and that "light perpetual may shine upon them," when we have been specifically assured that God's redeemed people already enjoy "peace" and "light"? To pray that they may be given what we are told they already have is derogatory to the work of Christ and incompatible with Christian assurance.

[6]The prayer of consecration in the communion service.

[7]D. M. Lloyd-Jones, *The New Man: An Exposition of Romans 6* (London: Banner of Truth, 1972), p. 264.

[8]Handley Moule, *Thoughts on Christian Sanctity* (London: Seeley, 1888), pp. 13-15.

[9]Ibid., p. 16.

[10]See *Truth, Error and Discipline* (London: Vine Books, 1978), a pamphlet produced by and for the Church of England Evangelical Council.

[11] J. C. Ryle, *Principles for Churchmen*, 4th ed. (London: Hunt, 1900).

[12]In 1981 J. I. Packer picked up Ryle's memorable phrase and wrote *A Kind of Noah's Ark? The Anglican Commitment to Comprehensiveness*, as a companion piece to his earlier study *The Evangelical Anglican Identity Problem: An Analysis* (Oxford: Latimer House, 1978).

[13]*The Fulness of Christ: The Church's Growth into Catholicity*, a report presented to the archbishop of Canterbury (London: SPCK, 1960), pp. 7-8.

[14]Alec Vidler, *Essays in Liberality* (London: SCM Press, 1957), p. 166.

[15]From J. I. Packer's essay "Taking Stock in Theology," in *Evangelicals Today*, ed. John C. King (Cambridge: Lutterworth, 1973), p. 17.

[16]John V. Taylor, *The Go-Between God* (London: SCM Press, 1972), p. 3.

[17]John Stott, ed., *Making Christ Known: Historic Mission Documents from the Lausanne Movement, 1974-1989* (Grand Rapids: Eerdmans, 1996), p. 238.

[18]William Temple, *Readings in St. John's Gospel* (1945; Macmillan, 1955), p. 130.

[19]Harry R. Boer, *Pentecost and Missions* (Cambridge: Lutterworth, 1961), p. 210.

[20]The Grand Rapids Report (1982), in *Making Christ Known*, ed. John Stott (Grand Rapids: Eerdmans, 1996), pp. 181-82.

[21]John Wimber, *Power Evangelism* (London: Hodder & Stoughton, 1985), p. 117.

[22]Ibid., p. 117.

[23]Ibid., p. 102.

[24]Stott, *Making Christ Known*, p. 238.

[25]It will be clear from this definition of *revival* as a supernatural and sovereign visitation of God that I am not alluding to "organizing a revival" (i.e., an evangelistic mission), an expression of very human origin still in use in some parts of the United States.

[26]Johannes Blauw, *The Missionary Nature of the Church* (1962; Grand Rapids: Eerdmans, 1974), p. 89.

Conclusion: The Challenge of the Evangelical Faith

[1]*Letter to Diognetus* 5.5.8.

[2]Rob Warner enlarges on some of these, and on others, in his chapter "Fracture Points," in Clive Calver and Rob Warner, *Together We Stand* (London: Hodder & Stoughton, 1996), pp. 60-93.

[3]So John T. Wilkinson in his introductory essay to *The Reformed Pastor* (London: Epworth,

1939), p. 31. The original Latin version of the proverb was *in necessariis unitas, in non-necessariis libertas, in omnibus caritas.*

[4]Alister McGrath, *Church of England Newspaper,* April 17, 1998.

[5]R. P. Martin, *Philippians,* Tyndale New Testament Commentary (Grand Rapids: Eerdmans, 1959), p. 86.

[6]A full account of the ten martyrs is given in Andrew Chandler, ed., *The Terrible Alternative* (London: Cassell, 1998).

Scripture Index

104:30, 87
119:97, 87
119:103, 87
119:105, 44

Ecclesiastes
12:9-10, 49

Genesis
1:2, 87
9:6, 72

Isaiah
1:10, 40
1:20, 47
6:3, 37, 43
28:13, 42
29:13, 94
53, 28
55:8-11, 41

Exodus
3:6, 71
4:1-9, 106
35:30, 87

Leviticus
17:11, 42

Jeremiah
1:1-9, 47
1:4, 40
6:14, 72
8:11, 72
31:33, 96

Numbers
6:22, 43

Deuteronomy
6:4, 43

Ezekiel
1:28, 71
13:10, 72
36:27, 93, 96

Judges
17:6, 64
18:1, 64
19:1, 64
21:25, 64

Daniel
10:12, 54

1 Samuel
3:10, 53

Matthew
3:11, 90
5:6, 99
5:10, 120
5:48, 98
10:37, 113
11:25, 44, 53, 124
16:17, 44
18:1-4, 123
28:18, 55
28:19, 90

1 Kings
17—18, 106

Ezra
1, 48

Psalms
91:4, 19

Mark
4:4, 65
7:1-13, 56
7:6, 94
7:20-23, 74
8:31, 68
8:34, 81
9:12, 68
9:31, 68
10:13-16, 124
10:34, 68
10:45, 68

Luke
1:1-4, 48
2:22-23, 47
3:8, 113
4:14, 64
10:39, 53
24:25-27, 28
24:32, 57
24:44-46, 28

John
1:16, 32
3:3, 89
3:5, 90
3:5-8, 89
3:7, 89, 91
7:37-39, 103
12:23, 68
12:27, 68
14:16, 32
14:17, 93
15:5, 124
15:18, 120
16:7, 92
16:8-11, 89
16:12-13, 57
16:14-15, 88

Acts
1:5, 95

2:22, 106
2:25-31, 28
2:33, 31, 95
2:38-39, 95
2:42, 100
3:21, 47
5:41, 120
8:31, 59
14:17, 37
16:11, 116
16:12, 112
17:23, 36
17:24-25, 37
17:31, 26
18:4, 29
18:23, 114
20:28, 102
26:14, 89
26:25, 115

Romans
1:19-20, 37
1:20, 38
1:32—2:2, 37
2:1, 38
3:24, 77, 130
3:28, 78
5:1, 78, 130
5:5, 94
5:6-10, 76
5:8, 69
5:9, 77
5:15-17, 130
6, 131
6:10, 30
6:23, 130
7:22, 87
8, 96
8:1, 77
8:3, 77
8:3-4, 96
8:7, 87
8:9, 88, 93

8:13, 97
8:15-16, 88, 94
8:23, 108
8:25, 109
15:4, 64
16:25, 114

1 Corinthians
1:17, 26
1:19-21, 36
1:20, 26
1:24, 26
1:31, 126
2:1, 26
2:1-5, 25
2:2, 26
2:3, 27
2:6, 26
2:7, 26
2:7-10, 36
2:13, 42
6:19, 93
10:1-5, 100
10:1-11, 63
10:11, 64
10:16, 117
12:3, 88
14:12, 102
15:1-2, 29
15:1-5, 27
15:2, 28
15:3, 27, 69
15:3-4, 28
15:11, 28

2 Corinthians
1:22, 108
3:18, 32, 79
5:5, 108
5:11, 115
5:19, 75
7:1, 98
12:12, 106

13:14, 100

Galatians
1:4, 69
1:6, 118
1:15-16, 44
2:11-17, 78
2:16, 78
2:17, 77
2:20, 80
3:1, 82
3:6-14, 75
3:13, 75
4:6, 88
4:14, 58
5, 96
5:6, 78
5:11, 83
5:16, 98
5:22-23, 32
5:24, 80
6:12, 83
6:14, 67, 71, 80

Ephesians
1:7, 69
1:14, 108
1:17, 32, 44
2:8-10, 78
2:20, 61
3:14, 32
3:16-17, 93
3:18, 8
4:1, 113
4:14, 114
4:30, 93
5:18, 99
6:10-17, 114

Philippians
1, 121
1:7, 115
1:9, 32

1:16, 115
1:20-26, 112
1:27, 111, 112, 114, 116
1:27-30, 112
1:28, 119
1:29, 119
2:1, 100
2:2, 116
2:9-11, 55
3:9, 78
3:12, 98
3:18, 76
3:20, 113

Colossians
1:10, 113
1:12-14, 130

1 Thessalonians
2:12, 113
2:13, 40
4:1, 32
4:7-8, 96
4:9-10, 32

1 Timothy
2:5-6, 69

2 Timothy
2:7, 54
3:5, 94
3:12, 120
3:16, 47

Titus
2:5, 113
2:10, 113

Hebrews
1:1, 42, 47
1:1-3, 39
1:2, 39

6:4-5, 108
7:27, 31
10:19-22, 69
11:32, 64

James
3:9, 72

1 Peter
2:21, 120
3:18, 31, 69
4:13, 120

2 Peter
1:19, 44
1:21, 47, 87
3:16, 59
3:18, 32

1 John
2:3, 94
2:5, 94
2:18, 118
3:2, 80
3:6, 98
3:9, 98
3:14, 94
3:19, 94
4:10, 69
4:13, 94
5:18, 98
5:19, 94

Jude
3, 30

Revelation
1, 38
1:17, 71
2:10, 121
4:8, 43
5:9, 69
5:12, 76

John Stott Ministries

The vision of John Stott Ministries (JSM) is to see majority world churches served by conscientious pastors who sincerely believe, diligently study, relevantly apply and faithfully expound the Word of God. For over thirty years JSM's Langham programs have helped burgeoning non-Western churches to balance *growth* with *depth*. Three key programs help majority world church leaders disciple their congregations toward greater spiritual maturity.

JSM-Langham Scholarships have enabled more than 120 majority world church leaders to study theology at the postgraduate level in the West. Upon completion of their degrees, these church leaders have returned home to train the next generation of pastors in their countries.

JSM-Langham Preaching Seminars gather pastors for instruction in biblical preaching and teaching. These seminars provide intensive training for pastors largely unschooled in Bible exposition, bringing greater skill and clarity to their preaching.

JSM-Langham Literature works with seminaries and Bible colleges in over seventy countries to give needed books to tens of thousands of pastors, many of whom before had nearly empty bookshelves.

You can participate in the global church. Find out more by visiting JSM at <www.johnstott.org> or contacting JSM at <info@johnstott.org>.